Swadhisthana Chakra

WORLD YOGA CONVENTION 2013
GANGA DARSHAN, MUNGER, BIHAR, INDIA
23rd–27th October 2013

Swadhisthana Chakra

Rishi Nityabodhananda

Yoga Publications Trust, Munger, Bihar, India

© Bihar School of Yoga 2013

All rights reserved. No part of this publication may be reproduced, transmitted or stored in a retrieval system, in any form or by any means, without permission in writing from Yoga Publications Trust.

The terms Satyananda Yoga® and Bihar Yoga® are registered trademarks owned by International Yoga Fellowship Movement (IYFM). The use of the same in this book is with permission and should not in any way be taken as affecting the validity of the marks.

Printed by Yoga Publications Trust
    First edition 2013

ISBN: 978-93-81620-86-1

Publisher and distributor: Yoga Publications Trust, Ganga Darshan, Munger, Bihar, India.

Website: www.biharyoga.net
        www.rikhiapeeth.net

Printed at Thomson Press (India) Limited, New Delhi, 110001

Dedication

*In humility we offer this dedication to
Swami Sivananda Saraswati, who initiated
Swami Satyananda Saraswati into the secrets of yoga.*

Contents

Introduction	1
1. Obstacle to Kundalini's Ascent	5
2. Swadhisthana and Samskaras	9
3. Understanding Swadhisthana	22
4. Awakening Swadhisthana	26
5. The Six-Petalled Lotus	36
6. Vrittis Related to Swadhisthana	40
7. Image and Symbology	46
8. Planes of Experience	69
9. Preparation for Swadhisthana Sadhana	76
Bibliography	95

Introduction

We will begin with an explanation of kundalini from a historical perspective. Nobody knows from where the idea first came, or who the original kundalini yogi was. Before the creation of language, before people could communicate to each other with words, they would manage with sounds, such as bird sounds, lion sounds or deer sounds, and their sounds had meanings such as, "Watch out, a lion's coming!" or "There's a nice bird over there; we might be able to catch it and eat it." This information comes to us from TV documentaries on anthropological studies relayed to us ordinary, non-experts by science journalists. We don't know if they are right or wrong; their information is evolving, it is theoretical and continues to evolve as each new bit of evidence is dug up. Thousands of years ago, the psychology of man was different. Charles Breaux, a recognized author, psychologist and kundalini adept, and director of the Berkeley Holistic Health Center in the US, writes in his book *Journey into Consciousness* that ancient people were more focused on intuitive abilities to source their information. For evidence, he points to the shape of ancient skulls indicating an emphasis in rear brain development rather than the modern, frontal lobe and forward thinking emphasis.

Since ancient times, people have been investigating the space within the body using their psychic vision and they have discovered that life is supported by an energy system. When they looked inside, they saw a myriad of sparks which they called 'prana'. When they looked more carefully at those sparks of prana, they noticed that the prana formed particular paths and was flowing in particular stream-like directions called *nadis*. These experiences of ancient sages were recorded in texts. *Hatha Yoga Pradipika* (4:18) and other tantric texts say that there are 72,000 nadis. They did not count this number; they knew it intuitively. The *Shiva Samhita* states that there are 350,000 nadis, which is five times more than the number mentioned in *Hatha Yoga Pradipika*. It seems *Shiva Samhita* considers subsequent branches of nadis, and from these there are an infinite number of subsequent branches. The *Kshurikopanishad* (17b) also mentions: *Dva-saptati-sahasrani pratinadisu taitilam* – "In each of the 72,000 nadis there is a material which is like oil."

Many nadis have been named, and their functions are understood to be that of energizing parts of the physical system. This knowledge is not confined to Indian teachings. It is also included in Japanese and Chinese schools where it is incorporated into the practice of acupuncture, which in turn is based on the original Indian schools of marma therapy. All this information is available in fine detail in the ayurvedic shastras. Now, of those thousands of nadis, fourteen are considered important, and of these the three most important are ida, pingala and sushumna.

When adepts looked at these flow lines or nadis inside the body, they noticed that they formed clusters on the spinal column which whirled like wheels and they were termed *chakras*. At the base of the body between the urinary and excretory passages there is a cluster they called *mooladhara chakra*; at the lowest tip of the spine there is another cluster called *swadhisthana chakra*; behind the navel there is a cluster called *manipura chakra*; in the spine around the middle of the chest there is a cluster called *anahata chakra*; in the spine behind the throat is another called *vishuddhi chakra*, and at the top of the spine behind the eyebrow centre is another cluster called *ajna chakra*. All these clusters were seen during meditation.

Looking at the clusters of flowing prana more carefully, the adepts noticed that they created a fantastic pattern of beautiful flowers. At the lowest chakra, at mooladhara, there were four perfect petals created by the flow of prana. These flowers aren't like the flowers in the external world; they don't have a smell, like a rose or a lotus, and they don't have a stamen or pollen. They're not that kind of flowers. These are flowers formed by the flow of energy, and when the energy flows it produces light. At each chakra point it gives a characteristic pattern. Why? It is because God cast an amazingly clear and beautiful mould and every human has these characteristic patterns within.

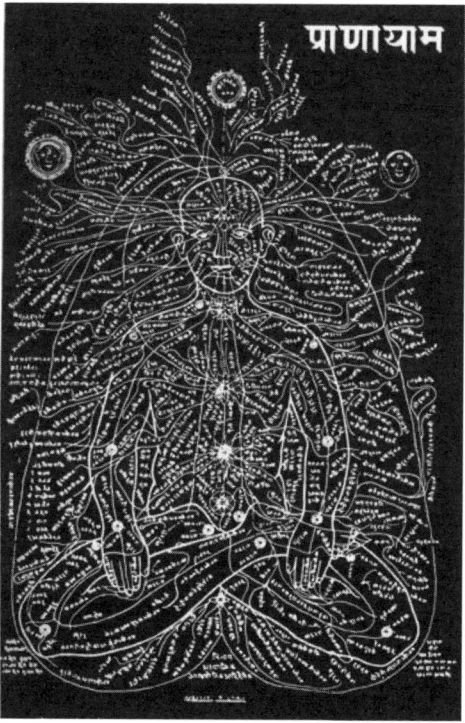

The network of nadis

We can look at it to be part of our makeup, our personal makeup, from which our outer personality comes. This is the basis of our kundalini yoga study. At the lowest level residing in mooladhara chakra is Ma Kundalini, primordial energy having the appearance of a snake and wound into three and a half coils. She's trying to come up. Sometimes Ma Kundalini comes up, looks around, opens her mouth a little, pokes her forked tongue out a little and wants to ascend, but there is no way. It is impossible for her to ascend and she returns to rest in mooladhara. Here we are, aspirants of yoga, and we want to know: Why can't we wake up and move out of mooladhara and ascend to the level of swadhisthana? This is the subject of this discussion.

1
Obstacle to Kundalini's Ascent

Why can't kundalini pass through swadhisthana? What is the problem? When kundalini is at mooladhara our consciousness is instinctive. It's our animal nature. Pavlov's psychological studies on dogs demonstrate this point. Give a dog a prize, a bit of food, and it will always think that it will get rewarded for repeating the same behaviour. That's about the level of mooladhara: 'Where's the food?' 'Where's the house?' 'Where is the security for the appetites in life?'

The source of our basic mooladhara actions lie in the mind, and the mind is at that level of consciousness when kundalini begins to energize swadhisthana chakra. The source of our personality is swadhisthana. At the level of swadhisthana we are aware of the mind. There is the mental aspect which manifests in swadhisthana as dissatisfaction, meaning that we start to become bombarded by thoughts and troubles; we start to have a lot of things going on and we think, 'Oh, I have this, but it's not enough.' 'I don't have that and I want it.' 'I want this and I want that.' 'I want this taste.' 'Oh, I only have ordinary food today, but I want that taste.' At the swadhisthana level of consciousness, we can begin to explore the depths of the mind and ultimately unravel the mystery that explains our behaviour: our drives that are expressed through our actions.

Deep in the unconscious mind is a self-created identity, the *ahamkara* or ego principle. Ahamkara tries to express itself in every facet of our life. Swami Sivananda called it the little 'I'. It is a creation and we can't get out of it. It's a myth; you open the eyes and what do you see? Well, you certainly see something and who sees it? 'I' do. Something goes on the tongue; who tastes it? 'I' do. You don't say, "The tongue tastes it and I am the witness," you say, "More sweets! I want more sweets." The 'I' is always screaming, it's always screaming; it's a little kid and it's in there. It always tries to get bigger and better and more, because this 'I' wants to exist, it wants to be, and it is deep in the unconscious at the swadhisthana level of mind. It is that part of the mind which can be contacted through swadhisthana chakra: the 'I'.

Meaning of swadhisthana
Swadhisthana means one's own abode, one's own place, and if we can loosen the bonds of ignorance in swadhisthana chakra through mental analysis and *vairagya*, letting go of our attachment to objects of desire, kundalini can find her way out of mooladhara into swadhisthana. She can ascend like a coiled spring being released just a little. Kundalini wants to ascend, but we have created so many illusions and traps and distortions associated with 'I' that she is blocked.

"Swadhisthana was once the seat of kundalini shakti," Swami Satyananda writes, "and due to a fall in consciousness, kundalini came to rest in mooladhara." At one time, of course, we were all angels; our nature was beyond the gunas. It was a golden age when there was no need for deceit or dishonesty. Why do we deceive, why are we dishonest? Because 'I' wants something. The shopkeeper says, "No, no, this product is expensive because it is the best quality available", to which I retort, "It looks just as big and shiny as the cheaper ones" and the shopkeeper's response is, "Oh no, don't you know the old adage, 'You get what you pay for'?" He's being dishonest, because 'I' wants more money. The hunger for expansion leads 'I' to hunger for more wealth, more fame, a higher position, a better reputation, more adoration. The unconscious source of lustful desires is based on ahamkara wanting to reproduce and ensure it will not be extinguished in death. The reproductive aspect of ahamkara is often distorted and takes a disproportionate share of our awareness.

Another meaning of swadhisthana is expressed in *Rudra Yamala*. Swadhisthana gets its name from the root *swa*, one's own innate, real force, soul, self. It is the place or abode of the *para linga* or supreme symbol. So, swadhisthana means 'my own place is the highest consciousness which is the para linga, the linga which is beyond all lingas'.

When we see no gain in gain and we see that desire is just the demand of ahamkara, and there is no sense of loss when we lose, when our mind is equal in all situations, then kundalini can pass through swadhisthana. However, there's more to discuss before we come to that point.

Success, a spiritual distraction

The ancient texts tell us that there was a golden age when the seat of kundalini was higher. Now the whole society has changed. Presently, we are very good at making iPhones and iPads and Samsung Galaxies called smart phones. We can send spacecraft to Mars. Some people have become creative geniuses and many are recognized by the whole world. There are people with great innovative skills who have brought new products to the world. They are presidents of the biggest companies in the world, acclaimed around the world. Yet, with all their genius, these people leave the world with a strong karma. In their next birth, their mind will probably focus on a path to becoming a recognized genius. In order to transcend this identity, they will have to avoid being a slave to the drive for success. That drive is a great tension and the consequence is further tension to maintain the 'number one' position. All because ahamkara wants to exist and wants to be the best, the most famous. Mulla Nasruddin, a famous Turkish poet and sage, was asked what it is like to be on the top rung of the ladder of success. He replied, "I have slaved hard and I have found the road to success no easy matter. I started at the bottom. I worked twelve hours a day. I perspired. I fought. I took abuse. I did things I did not approve of, yet I kept right on climbing the ladder." "And now, of course, you are a success, Mulla?" prompted the questioner. "No, I would not say that," replied Nasruddin with a laugh. "Just quote me as saying that I have become an expert at climbing ladders."

Kundalini will not be able to pass through swadhisthana so long as the focus is driven by the demands of ahamkara. Such a person could be stuck in swadhisthana for a long time to come, due to that image of 'I' that he has to create. Closer home, we see yoga teachers who wish to become famous on the international stage, become five-star swamis and be recognized by so many people. It is very difficult to get out of that impression unless we have a guru who can redirect our duties so that we are forced to adjust to a life without fame and adulation. It all has to do with the 'I'.

With the passage of time, and due to tamasic influences and the changes in society, the level of conscious awareness has continued to fall as the focus on the importance of 'I' has grown. As a result, kundalini has now gone below swadhisthana and rests in mooladhara. It is easy to get out of mooladhara. There are not many limitations in mooladhara. Swadhisthana is the big stumbling block that we have to get through.

2
Swadhisthana and Samskaras

Life is our teacher, whether it be in sannyasa training, in our yoga life, or in the knocks and difficulties and troubles of worldly life; we learn to let go and are able to come through swadhisthana. If kundalini fell any lower than mooladhara, however, we would be worse off than animals. We would be less evolved than animals, less than insects. Swadhisthana is the basis of individuality; it is the 'I'. It is also the storehouse of our *samskaras*, the mental impressions embedded within the mind, within the subtle body, which we have to look at deeply.

Samskaras influence every aspect of our lives, yet we are unaware of them because they lie deep in the unconscious. By awakening swadhisthana, we become aware of unconscious aspects of ourselves, and through this process we continue trying to learn about our samskaras. Just as we can watch TV and remain unaware of electronic processes going on behind the screen, in the same way, we can see our thoughts, our hatreds, our envies, our jealousies and our prejudices and yet we are unaware of the source of these imperfections, for they are hidden in the unconscious part of our mind. They are the samskaras. If we're lucky, while doing japa and meditation or in dreams we can re-experience a samskara. The images and other sensory memories resurface into our conscious awareness and by re-experiencing a samskara, the mind is untethered from that binding impression and swadhisthana opens up that much more.

There was a swami in the ashram a long time ago when we lived in the old Bihar School of Yoga by the railway line. He was very energetic and constantly immersed in karma yoga, and practised a lot of meditation and kriya yoga. Then he entered a phase of lethargy. For weeks he couldn't find the energy to do anything, and then one day he received a big shock.

He was looking over the wall at the back of the ashram which overlooked the railway tracks. Every morning the locals would go there and squat on the railway lines for their toilet. They used the railway lines to keep themselves up off the ground a bit and then go to a nearby pond to clean themselves up. The wild pigs squealing with delight would come trotting over and they would clean it up. We used to refer to them as the cleaners from our public health department! The swami happened to see the pigs slurping up the filth and from the depths of his lethargy, he had a vision, at which he gave out an expression of disgust "Aaarrrgh!" He had experienced a shock, a shock of disgust. The disgust was not at what he saw with his eyes, but rather at the vision triggered by it. The event had brought up a samskara. When he was just eight years old, he was fishing with his father on a wharf. While he was fishing, the line went into the water and he thought he had a fish. His father said to him, "Pull it out." When the line came out, there was no fish on it. He said, "Dad, there's no fish on the hook." Then the hook dropped into the tin of worms and his father said, "Pull it out of the worms." He pulled it out too quickly and the whole bunch of worms hit his face. Suddenly, that swami who was so tired he could hardly do meditation was relieved of the problem and was restored to his previous energetic state, as he had relived that samskara. You have to re-experience or relive the samskara and sometimes it comes out like a little movie.

A similar incident occurred at the Dhanbad Ashram in India where I was stationed. While we were planting rice, the tractor got stuck up to the axle in the mud. I said, "Oh, I'll get it out." I jumped on the tractor and accelerated; however, instead of getting out of the bog it went deeper and deeper into the mud. Then some boys came up with a way to modify the tractor wheels to take the tractor through the water and mud. However, instead of the tractor going forward as it should have, due to all the stuff and weight behind it, the tractor's nose rose up first into *utthanpadasana*, stretched leg pose, then a little bit further into *ardha sarvangasana*, half-shoulder stand, then a little bit further into *poorna sarvangasana*, full shoulder stand, and finally fully over into *halasana*, plough pose, and I was stuck underneath. An urgent call went out to all the locals; they had to call people and try to get the tractor lifted up so I could be released. For twenty or thirty minutes I was stuck under the mud. I used my time under the tractor repeating my guru's name while my body went into shock with rapid breathing through my nose which was just above the water line. My mind was repeating, 'Swamiji, Swamiji, Swamiji', as efforts to release me continued. First, about twenty men lifted the tractor a little, but then it slipped and pressed down on me again. Finally, they lifted the tractor and my rescuers dragged me out. I came out backwards covered in mud with a couple of broken ribs. I was washed clean of all the mud and I was free and all right, but afterwards I realized I was not all right; I was traumatized.

What is it like to be traumatized? Suddenly you go from a clear, light mind to something like a faulty fluorescent tubelight. Something's not right. Everything works, you still have ten fingers, you can still see, but not everything is working as it should. This traumatized state continued for some time. One morning I just happened to squat down in a corner, and suddenly the whole event came out again like a movie. The people arriving, the tractor being lifted, the tractor slipping, the tractor coming down again on me, then the people lifting it again. All the voices were there: the sense of urgency of the rescue operation was there, then in my vision they dragged me out, hosed me down and poured buckets of water over me; I was full of mud and everything. Then I was out and I was okay. The miniature filmstrip of this experience ended. I had relived that traumatic experience and I was clear again. Suddenly the load that was on my back was eliminated. That was just the elimination of one samskara. How many thousands and thousands of samskaras are we loaded with?

Sri Aurobindo was a genius. He would read a box of books a day. His first yogic experience of clearing the mind and being liberated was in prison. He met a guru while he was in political prison and his guru is mentioned in his writings. The guru said, "Stop trying to get knowledge from the books; you've got it all within. Empty your mind." In his autobiography, Sri Aurobindo writes that he started by looking at thoughts. At first one thought came, then another, and another, and after some time he witnessed thousands of thoughts simultaneously streaming past his mind's eye, and then the thoughts came to an end. He writes, "It was my great debt to my guru, Lele, that he showed me this. 'Sit in meditation,' he said, 'but do not think, look only at your mind. You will see thoughts coming into it; before they can enter, throw them away until your mind is capable of entire silence.' I had never before heard of thoughts coming visibly into the mind from outside, but I did not think either of questioning the truth of the possibility, I simply sat down and did it. In a moment my mind became as silent as a windless air on a high mountain summit, and then it was one thought and then another coming in a concrete way from outside. I flung them away before they could enter and take hold of the brain and in three days I was free. From that moment, in principle, the mental being in me became a free Intelligence, a Universal Mind, not limited to the narrow circle of personal thoughts as a labourer in a thought factory, but a receiver of knowledge from all the hundred realms of being, and free to choose what it willed in this vast sight-empire and thought-empire."

After three days, Sri Aurobindo's whole mind was empty. He was an advanced soul, a great guru. He had the capacity to practise antar mouna in that way, and he let all the suppressed samskaras, the suppressed experiences in the mind out, and he was relieved. Why are they suppressed? We don't like distressing experiences, therefore we don't like to remember them. This is our childhood coding. Immature minds reject awful, painful memories, thus samskaras remain suppressed. Mature minds can accept distressing experiences. If something awful happens to you, you say, "Hmm, I don't want to think about it." It makes you feel bad, therefore it remains suppressed. The aspirant of yoga is mature and keen to face the content of the mind so you have to let them all out. Samskaras have to be released for Ma Kundalini to pass through swadhisthana.

Karmas
Samskaras are embedded. We seem to be born with them. Lord Buddha was born into a royal family which was spiritually ignorant. They were immersed in the materialistic philosophy of luxury and pleasantness being the ultimate goals of life, yet his seemingly inborn drive to pursue a spiritual goal involving austere sadhanas compelled him to continue. These embedded samskaras are karmas.

Jesus Christ was the son of a carpenter, yet his inborn drive was for a real relationship with God his Father in heaven. Christ's life was a manifestation of his embedded samskaras, his karmas. Astrologically, his karmas can be seen in his natal chart. This chart shows that the person born at that time was in for great difficulties in his personality. The world of Christ was in opposition to his views. He was a revolutionary. His chart is full of conflict except for just two aspects: his duty towards expansion of how the world relates to him, and his capacity for unusual psychic vision. Both of these aspects made it easy for him to pursue his path to establish a faith that was controversial at that time. The other karmas were difficult ones and almost each aspect of the chart is in conflict, pain and suffering. Yet Christ could walk on water, feed the multitude with a few loaves and fish, and bring the dead back to life. He was a siddha whose immersion in the divine transcended his suffering. He went through his karmas, yet his identity was focused on the divine and not on his suffering. He is known for his compassion, not for his problems. This path is a path which transcended his individual ahamkara identity and kundalini could pass through swadhisthana. Thus Christ's life has become an example for millions to follow in their efforts to lead a divine life.

What can we learn from this as aspirants of kundalini yoga trying to pass through swadhisthana? We can learn to accept our karmas and live through them while having an unwavering connection with our divine origins.

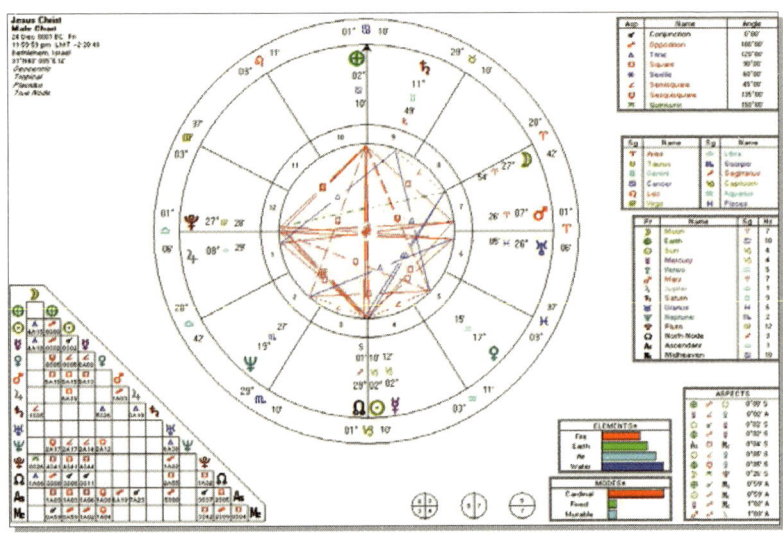

Jesus Christ's birth chart

Everyone has karma

Every person has an enormous number of karmas. Whether you are the greatest saint, the purest person, even if you are very vegetarian or vegan and you never say anything negative at all, deep within your karmas are still a mixture of positive and negative aspects. Those who know anything about astrology will be aware that everyone has Saturn in their chart. Everyone has Pluto in their chart. At this moment in time, Pluto in Capricorn is exposing all the corruption in the financial corporations worldwide. Also being exposed is corruption in administrations, governments and religious organizations. Suppressed illegal criminal activities in major organizations worldwide are also being exposed. Pluto is the planet of the unconscious mind, and everyone has Pluto in their chart. Everyone certainly has a sun sign, the sun in their chart. Nobody is free from the influences of all the planets, and where are these planets? They are our own minds. They're not just out there in space; they are also within.

Tony Nader received his PhD in the area of Brain and Cognitive Science from the Massachusetts Institute of Technology (MIT) in the US, where he was also a visiting physician at the institute's Clinical Research Centre. He did his post-doctoral work as a Clinical and Research Fellow in Neurology at the Massachusetts General Hospital, Harvard Medical School. His book, *Human Physiology*, demonstrates the link between the macrocosmic planets and signs, and their concomitant existence in various parts of the brain. This book was his first and was his submission to MIT for his PhD where it was accepted by his peers. There is a part of the brain which is Saturn; it is a physical, anatomical part of the brain. These things are all there and it just goes to show that everyone is made up of a whole host of karmas and samskaras. No one is free until they can transcend.

Swami Satyananda writes in *Kundalini Tantra*, "The unconscious principle of swadhisthana should never be considered inactive or dormant. It is far more dynamic and powerful than normal consciousness. When shakti enters swadhisthana, there is an overwhelming experience of this unconscious state and this has to be faced. Sadhakas with good samskaras can traverse the ocean of the unexplored

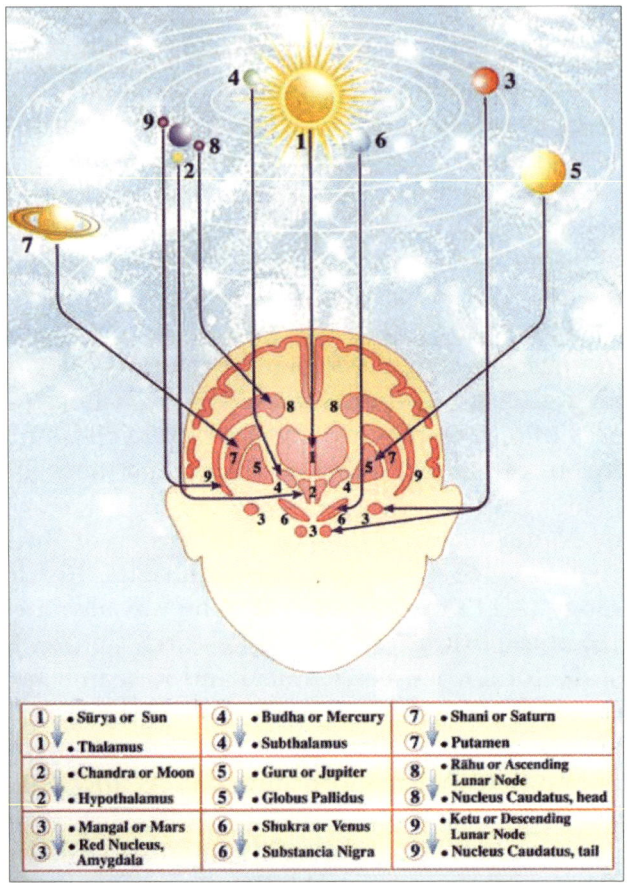

A coronal section of the brain with its internal structures including the basal ganglia, the thalamus, the hypothalamus, the subthalamus, etc., and their one-to-one relation to the nine planets of the solar system.

unconscious and accept it. The dynamic and powerful path is to be crossed through a disciplined life without limits.

"Break the limitations of sleep requirements, do the jobs that the mind rejects, open up the possibility that whatever you do in this way is expanding the awareness of the unconscious, then the path and the nadis are ready for Ma Kundalini's passage through swadhisthana. The lure of taste, the lure of sensuality is a constant demand in everyone's life. It is our addiction to life in the world. If you alter life's path to fulfil that want, you will never have enough, and your whole life will be captivated by wanting."

Swadhisthana is different from mooladhara, which is the manifest expression of that unconscious. In mooladhara, the karmas of the lower stages of our evolution are manifested in the form of anger, greed, jealousy, passion, love, hatred, and so on. In mooladhara, we work out that karma, manifesting and expressing it overtly. At the level of swadhisthana, there is no conscious activity or manifestation. If somebody is running after you, yelling and shouting and saying something like "You stole my roti!" or "You stole my dhoti!" then you know, 'Hey, he's talking from mooladhara. That state of consciousness, that's just ordinary animal consciousness.' When you turn around and say, "Think about it, my friend", it is a sign that mooladhara has awakened and swadhisthana is being traversed.

Karmas can be understood to be psychological in nature, and they relate to different ganglia of nerves in the brain, different parts of the brain. The macrocosmic view is from the point of view of the planets. Most of our karmas are fixed: personality, nationality, body type, nervous disposition, and others. We are born with these characteristics as a result of previous choices.

Personal experiences

Karmas living in the unconscious do not allow the ascending kundalini to pass through. The problem is there, but unrecognizable. Why is it unrecognizable? What happens when you have a dream of unconscious stuff; do you always know what you are dreaming about? The other night I had a dream that I was showing off my T-shirt to someone, and it was made out of a British flag. I'm Australian! I was showing off my British flag T-shirt to somebody. Then I looked up at him, and he was wearing exactly the same T-shirt! What on earth was that about? I have no idea.

Things change inside the ocean of the mind. If you were to drop something, say a gun, into the ocean and you pulled it out some time later, it would be unrecognizable. As a matter of fact, I know a story about a gun and this actually happened. Some years ago, there was a court case involving some corrupt police and the evidence was a lot of guns. They went to a place called the Hawkesbury River and threw the guns into the river, probably with the thought, 'This will get rid of the evidence and they'll never catch us now.' Some years later, a whistleblower, an informant, exposed them. Investigators hauled the guns up and the operation was shown on TV. What we saw on TV was unrecognizable at first glance; however, since we knew what they were, we could sort of tell that they were once guns. Now badly corroded and caked in mud, the guns could still be identified as guns, having roughly the same shape.

In the same way, our samskaras change shape in the ocean of the mind. A personal example: I have never seen a pig snorting at a gate outside, but I've seen it inside, internally. Where does it come from? It is probably some distortion of a bully I went to school with. He pushed me around and he gave me trouble, and I thought somewhere in the back of my mind when I was little, 'He's a pig.' I don't know for sure; I'm only guessing now. So, we don't often understand the symbology of the samskara, but we understand the feeling and impression. We understand that whatever comes out must be witnessed, as it is, without understanding it. This is how to traverse the ocean of samskara. This is only one of the things we have to work with; there are many more things to cross. Swadhisthana is extremely difficult to cross. We have created so many boundaries, so many limitations, and we're going to have to deal with them.

Individuals and desires

The unconscious material, the samskara and the karma is there, but it is unrecognizable. Swami Satyananda writes, "Therefore, awakening of swadhisthana results in a very confusing and insane mind." If you're sitting in the comfort of your home and the television is there with all your channels, the fridge is there with exactly what you want, the cupboards are there filled with exactly what you want, the chair is there exactly where and how you would be comfortable and the bed is there exactly how you want it, you won't feel anything. The mind is not struggling with the worldly choices you can make, "I'll have this or that, I'll have skim milk or I'll have whole milk", and the list goes on. It is only when you don't get what you want, such as under conditions of self-restraint or discipline when there is no fridge full of delicious snacks, or when you come to an ashram and there is no telly, no fridge, no choice of food. You will likely never experience it out there in the comfort of your home, but when you are denied those things, it is an opportunity for the samskaras to exhibit themselves. People who used to enjoy a cold beer in the hot weather unexpectedly experience cans of beer floating past their minds when hot weather beats down on them. They start seeing the little frosty bubbles on the glass, and they say, "I would do anything for a glass of beer." The guru challenges you, he says, "No, you've got this duty, and you've got that duty, and you can't go out the gate, and you can't do this, and you can't do that." Wait two years, three years; you forget about beer! You forget about sweet fruits and Continental cheeses.

    The mind relaxes from its external pursuits. You exhaust the samskaras one by one. There are so many things that surface. Be patient. Bear them bravely and know that the samskaras will exhaust themselves. It can be very confusing. Sometimes, for example, if you are in *mouna*, silence, doing a lot of meditation and hardly moving, such as during the practice of *udasina mouna,* that indifferent, passive state where you are simply looking down at your toenails all the time only chanting the mantra, the samskaras in the mind can come out so fast, and be so confusing, that your only grasp with sanity is to be able to count the fingers, 'Ah. I've got ten fingers, at least I know that's true.' Inside it is also confusing, and you say, '*Om* . . . ah, that mantra, that's *Om*, at least there's something I know.' However, the world, your sanity, your security system, the 'I' is nowhere to be found. It's a problem! Thank God we have a guru who is able to help us understand that we are going through these confusing states and getting through swadhisthana. We all want to evolve and that's why we're looking for answers.

Evolved beings

If we do not want to be held in the perpetual jaws of jealousy and anger and want to free ourselves from the grip of karmas, we need a guru who understands this confusing state. Lord Buddha experienced Mara, the demonical temptress. She can be a big snake, or a naked woman, or a grotesque person. Jesus Christ also faced huge temptations and these are the temptations coming out of swadhisthana. Now, when we talk to people about this topic, they always talk about swadhisthana and sex, swadhisthana and lust. Everybody says, "That's only swadhisthana stuff." You cannot just discount it like that. Lust is only one of the things and it's a strong one. It comes up as the temptress or tempter, if we want to give it a gender. Swami Satyananda writes, "Only those of strong will can survive the temptation, and we need vairagya to know there is no satisfaction through meeting or acting on these desires. Then kundalini passes through." This experience of temptation will always be there, yet once you pass through swadhisthana, the noose-like grip which makes you feel as if you are tied with a rope to those experiences and that you simply can't rise above and witness them, goes away. The temptation is always there, for *kundalini shakti*, the primal energy, manifests at different levels of consciousness in different ways. You don't lose the qualities of lower chakras having crossed over them to higher ones.

Even the ancient rishis were married and had children, illustrious children, wonderful children, genius and saintly children. Swami Satyananda writes beautifully in *Kundalini Tantra* about a swami's experience coming through swadhisthana: "I was sitting all night. Nothing but sex and sensual thoughts came to my mind. I dreamed of many women presenting themselves in their naked form, and my whole body was becoming hot and cold, hot and cold. Ultimately, I got a headache. At one point I thought my heart would collapse. Throughout the crisis, my guru's face would come like a glimpse. His face was stern and expressionless, and that used to bring my temperature back to normal. However, this confrontation I was having with a powerful side of my mind continued until morning. At last when morning came, I breathed a sigh of relief. But then, when I sat for meditation again in the evening, I had mixed feelings. I had fear in my mind and confidence as well. Day in and day out, the mind played its tricks on me. Then one night, Parvati came to me. Parvati is the shakti of Lord Shiva, and she is the Divine Mother. I knew she was Parvati, but because she looked so beautiful and she was wearing almost transparent clothing, I began to desire her. Rather than remembering she was the Divine Mother, my mind was more aware of the form behind the transparent apparel. Like a flash of lightning, my guru showed his face. I regained my senses and prayed, 'Mother, withdraw your maya. I can't face these experiences. You are the giver of liberation. You are the creator of illusion. You have the power to cast me back into the cycle of birth and rebirth, and you have the power to lift me from the quagmire of ignorance.' As I prayed, the tears rolled down my face. And I felt a cool breeze passing through my body. The panorama vanished, and I understood that kundalini had passed through swadhisthana and was now heading towards manipura."

3

Understanding Swadhisthana

Swadhisthana is located at the base of the spine, level with the coccyx. The *kshetram*, the chakra trigger point in front of the body, is level with the pubic bone. The location point corresponds with urinary and reproductive systems, and is related to the prostatic and utero-vaginal systems. You can see the kidneys there and the urinary system contains the kidneys, the left and right ureters and the bladder.

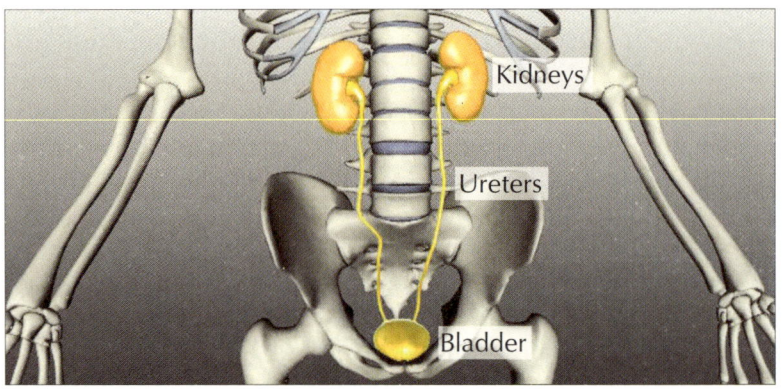

The location of the kidneys, the ureters and the bladder

Associated element

Mooladhara is an earth element and swadhisthana is a water element. Swadhisthana is the manifestation of the water element in us and it is connected with all our fluid systems. We are made up of five elements, the *pancha tattwas*: space, air, fire, water, and earth. The manifestation of our water element is swadhisthana, therefore the physical associations of swadhisthana are with water. Here we are discussing organs which produce fluids such as the urinary, reproductive, prostate, and utero-vaginal systems.

Physical and pranic relationship

There are connections between the nadis and the physical organs. Those who have been to acupuncturists will know that they insert needles all over the body. They are not pinning the body down, they are releasing tension and blockages in the pranic nadis and this gives physical benefits. I personally have been relieved of back problems, knee problems and digestive problems. I've even seen, through such treatments using laser acupuncture, that the fever of children will come down in minutes and chronic and so-called incurable problems are relieved. This emphasizes the associations between the physical, the pranic and the psychic systems. Through meditation, as a result of balancing the flow of prana in particular locations, we can bring about changes in the physical system. It works the other way around also. Through practice of particular physical postures, *asanas*, we can bring about changes in the psychic level and the flow of prana. In fact, this is one of the purposes of practising asana.

Thus, if we have a disorder or problem in the kidneys or in the reproductive system, we can visit doctors and specialists, but we should also do the practices for the energizing of swadhisthana. Then there are the endocrine functions: the testosterone and sperm cells, the prostate, the vagina and the mucous membranes, the ovaries and the egg cells and the oestrogen, the progesterone and the testosterone. The function of the endocrine system is to help in regulating the hormones secreted by the physical glands, and this system is also associated and influenced by the functioning of swadhisthana chakra. These are the physical associations linked with the psychic chakra.

This is all discussed in *Kundalini Tantra* by Swami Satyananda. There are a number of other relevant books available on this subject as well, although they don't deal with the physical aspect as much as in Swami Satyananda's text. *Laya Yoga* by Shyam Sundar Goswami is a very scholarly work, detailing and systematically presenting a vast collection of scriptural references from the Vedantas, Puranas, tantras and other rare manuscripts. It's a very good resource for accessing the ancient knowledge of kundalini.

Mistaken as spleen chakra

Swadhisthana is occasionally referred to as the 'spleen chakra'. The spleen is located in and slightly under the ribcage. A spiritual man by the name of Leadbeater, a member of Theosophical Society in the early 1900s with Annie Besant, Madame Blavatsky and others, started a society which has a large ashram in Chennai, India, and wonderful bookshops around the world. One of the original theosophists, Leadbeater wrote that the second chakra is the spleen chakra situated over the spleen, and he does not list swadhisthana at the lowest tip of the spine. Subsequent writers concluded the same; they all followed Leadbeater without looking into it deeply, and mistook the spleen chakra for swadhisthana. Although this may have been the experience of Leadbeater, the vast body of literature from ancient times clearly demonstrates that the second chakra is not at the spleen, but at the base of the spine, and its name is swadhisthana, not spleen. Finally, I came up with my own conclusion: it is not the spleen chakra. The spleen is shown below in Figure 5.

The spleen is located in the upper left of the abdomen, it aids in red blood cell formation, it is part of the lymph system and it is distant from swadhisthana. Now it is obvious that Leadbeater had an experience in the spleen and as a result he said the second chakra was in the spleen. He didn't call it swadhisthana; he called it the second chakra.

However, the tantras, the Puranas, the Upanishads, other classical texts and traditions tell us, via personal experience, that swadhisthana is at the tip of the tailbone. It is rather typical for people to have different experiences on a wide spectrum. Someone may feel a kind of vibration in their spinal column, maybe a thrilling psychic experience going up the spinal column, and they come tell you, since you are the teacher, "My kundalini is awakened." In fact, they are awakening an experience in sushumna nadi, possibly thrilling, possibly surprising, and possibly unusual, but not the kundalini experience.

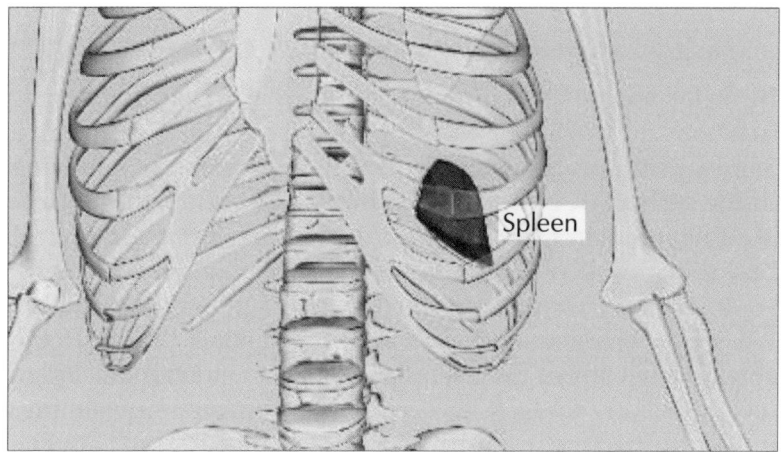

Location of the spleen

4
Awakening Swadhisthana

In order to awaken kundalini in its upward path, we must first awaken the chakras. After that, we awaken sushumna. *Sushumna nadi* is the path inside the spinal column, and lying inside sushumna is *chitrini nadi*, the nadi in which the chakras are formed. After awakening the chakras and the path, we can then awaken kundalini. Therefore, in our kundalini yoga sadhana, we must first work intensely on each chakra. We recite mantras and japa in each chakra. We perform concentration on each chakra. Some chakras are more sensitive than others. Some people may have intense feelings in swadhisthana and other people, nothing. It doesn't matter; sometimes anahata has feeling, sometimes manipura has intense feeling. When you chant *Om* in the chakras for instance, you can detect whether the chakra is awake or dormant. A good feeling usually vibrates in mooladhara, as mooladhara is usually awake.

Then we continue our investigation of swadhisthana. Is there a feeling, is it awake or not, nothing much or something there? What is awake? Are we consciously aware of the chakra? If we're aware of it, we know about it. We have connected our consciousness with that psychic part of the body just as we can awaken awareness of the hand, arm or leg and feel the difference between conscious and not-conscious in that part of the body. Similarly, by following the instructions in yoga nidra, "Right hand thumb, become aware of the right hand thumb . . ." we can awaken the top of the thumb, the knuckle, the base of the thumb, feel the whole thumb and then slowly become more and more aware of the thumb. In the same way, we can become aware of swadhisthana chakra. Of course, the thumb is a little easier and the chakra is a little more difficult as it is subtle. It is a subtle manifestation of the movement of prana and it takes some time to be able to establish proper awakening of the chakra. Awakening the chakra is not the same as awakening kundalini; this is just awakening the chakra and making it ready for sadhana.

The next step is the awakening of sushumna; you take the mantra up sushumna and back down again, up again and back down again. Then you decide, or your guru decides ,if you are ready for kundalini awakening. It is possible to have your kundalini awakened at this point. However, if you awaken the full force of kundalini shakti into swadhisthana chakra just now, the whole of your unconscious, karmas and samskaras that we discussed previously, unfold rather quickly. This opening up of the full storehouse of unconscious memory is more than confusing; it is overwhelming. You could start acting like a mad person. I have seen many people, including myself, who had ambitiously taken to this sadhana prematurely.

I used to live with one man who came back from the Himalayas where he had done intense sadhana for many years, prematurely. Due to his high aspirations, he quit his position as an engineer and lived as a sadhu in the Himalayas for many years, practising japa meditation and pranayama. He was constantly twitching; after years of meditation, he was constantly tense and twitching, worried and thinking. He thought there was nothing wrong with his mental state, yet in his spiritual zeal he had suppressed a host of worldly desires with one decision: to merge with infinite spiritual consciousness. Somehow, God led him to Swami Satyananda who immediately saw the problem. Swami Satyananda gave him the newspaper every day, *The Indian*

Nation, from Patna, India. He had to read the newspaper every day to bring him back down to earth, to stabilize him, to bring him into balance. I used to have a look at the newspaper and what was going on. It's a very ordinary paper, *The Indian Nation*, and not very interesting; however, he would read it and discuss Indian politics with me so I discovered the various views within Indian political parties and he became more stabilized.

Progressing in the right order
Kundalini sadhana should begin with ajna chakra. Swami Satyananda explains in *Kundalini Tantra*: "Although there are experiences of trance in other chakras, there is no merger of the individual ego with the cosmic ego. All throughout, you find you are trying to assert yourself behind all the experiences you are having; however, when ida and pingala unite with sushumna in ajna chakra, you lose yourself completely. I don't mean that you become unconscious. Your awareness expands and becomes homogeneous. Then individual awareness falls flat and you completely transcend the realm of duality. Thus, ajna chakra is a very important centre which you must experience in order to bring about purification of the mind. Once the mind is purified, the experience and awakening of the other chakras can proceed."

Awakening samskaras or becoming subject to karmas, past experiences, dreams, visions and all the unconscious matter is like driving at night without headlights. We'd crash all the time. Thus, we start with ajna chakra. Ajna chakra is the intuitive eye or the intuitive vision giving us the ability to see and to witness, rather than be enmeshed in unconscious matter as it unfolds. We have to be able to see where we are going when our inner eye is awakened rather than being controlled by every thought, vision and feeling. We can say, 'Ah, there's a thought. Oh, there is an awful experience. There is a violent experience. There's one with terrible feelings of guilt', and so on. When you have the intuitive eye, you have some perspective; you have the ability to be able to see from a distance. The problems aren't too close; you then have vision and you are able to see. That is why we start kundalini sadhana from ajna.

The little 'i' – a big obstacle for progress

Swami Satyananda has described it very nicely in *Kundalini Tantra*. Swadhisthana is the seat of the unconscious. At the depth of the unconscious is the 'i'. I prefer to call this the little 'i' that we have chosen to identify with. There is the superconscious, the wonderful superconscious, yet we choose to identify with that little 'i', a tiny, limited ahamkara, but that is our nature. It is our nature, it is our coding. It is in all of us and it is called *avidya*, ignorance and delusion. To identify with the little 'i' is avidya, and it is similar to a child who picks up a pretty bottle of poison and drinks it out of ignorance simply because it looks pretty. There is even a song about this little 'i' that Swami Sivananda sings:

> *Within you is the hidden God,*
> *Within you is immortal soul!*
> *Kill the little 'i'.*
> *Die to live.*
> *Lead the divine life.*
> *Within you is the fountain of joy.*
> *Within you is the ocean of bliss.*
> *Rest peacefully in your own atma,*
> *Drink the nectar of immortality.*

It is a nice idea to sing about. We can't, however, manage to get out of identification with the little 'i'. So, what is the secret? What is the way out of that limited 'i'? How do we get out of that 'i'? We get out by expanding it. This is Swami Satyananda's advice. We make it bigger and bigger so that the 'i' is no longer only interested in this limited self: 'My plate, my food, my mood, my bed, my worry.' We expand it, and we keep allowing our individual, limited 'i' expand so that my neighbour's 'i' is also my problem, my concern. We become part of each other's problems; we expand the 'i'. In this way, we become associated with more people, and more things outside of ourselves.

One morning, I began to eat a chappati left over from the previous night; it was sitting in the cupboard. I took a bite of it and suddenly I felt this electric nip on my lip! Then I looked at the chappati properly and saw a myriad of tiny ants. I thought, 'I'm having a fight with an ant. It wants the chappati and I want the chappati.' I went into an internal, philosophical debate. 'Should I be compassionate and take some chappati, put it over there and shake all the other ants off, or should I just kill them all and eat the lot?' It was a little incident, but nevertheless an example of the little things that we consider in life. Some people are extreme in their non-violence because they are so considerate of the existence of other living beings. We have to decide upon an appropriate path that does not limit the ordinary practicalities of a simple life.

This view of expanding the 'i' raises all kinds of objections. For expansion of the 'i' we do consider all others including the ants, and we have to be practical so that in considering others, we do not annihilate our capacity to function. The plant world is also a part of us which we can connect with and expand to. We can expand to the animal world. We can expand to little babies. We can expand to dogs and cats too, so that the welfare and needs of everything, including the plants, including the animals, including the ants that want my chappati, all of them are part of my 'i'. So, make the 'i' bigger and bigger, until it is unlimited. Then it is not a limitation any more; and we will be wiser.

At one stage, swadhisthana was the seat of kundalini. Actually, before swadhisthana, manipura was the seat of kundalini. Then as we passed through the various yugas, the consciousness of people descended. It became more rational, logical, more forward thinking and concerned with making a profit and generally more involved in expanding the establishment of ourselves. The whole consciousness of the world descended, and so did the seat of kundalini. Consciousness descends, and it is still descending.

As previously mentioned, swadhisthana is related to our unconscious storehouse of samskaras and karmas. The karmas are endless. Why have we come to this point in life of investigating swadhisthana chakra? Do we want to become sannyasins, spiritual aspirants or seekers? Do we want to become liberated and wise like the Buddha? Do we want to live under austere situations and strive for spiritual life? Was it just an idea? Or an accident of fate or something similar? Or was it something that just happened to you and you decided, 'One day, this is what I must do'? There is no status in gaining an understanding of swadhisthana, there is no money in it. You won't get a nice house out of it. What is the reason? Your karma; it is due to your driving search for deeper knowledge. Something each of us has, our own individual karma, which is embedded within us. At some stage in the past history of our soul we decided to make a move and try to establish a connection with the divine. Somehow we would try to do it and our various connections and associations have brought us here, to this situation, reading this book.

As an example, when I first went to India, I didn't know what a guru was. I thought he was a five-star eminent yoga teacher or I thought, 'Well, he must be some sort of yoga and meditation teacher.' I only came because I heard these gurus can put you deep into meditation and you can see higher realms. I said, 'Yes! I will go to India and discover deeper meditation so I can escape the problems of this world and live in a higher realm.' It was an escape route to a land of dreams, and I started having all these dreams about houses breaking up and things turning upside down, and different colours, and staircases going upside down and suddenly I was in Munger, India! Then I got a telegram about somebody who was sick in Delhi, and I suddenly didn't know what to do; I was stuck. Should I leave this life-changing opportunity I had arrived at? Just then I saw an eminent yoga teacher walking up and down at the other end of the old BSY; it was Swami Satyananda. I thought, 'I can't ask his advice, he is just a teacher.' Then he went away. I only had that thought and he went away. I learnt my lesson. I am a very slow learner. It took me years to work it out.

So what does this 'i' want? What does this ahamkara want? First of all, it wants to 'be'. It wants to be, it doesn't want to be extinguished. Take a look at a mosquito; it's got the same sort of idea. It does not have to be a very highly evolved thing to have an ahamkara. If you try to catch one, it will do everything in its power to escape, because the 'i' or ahamkara in a mosquito is desperate to survive. Cockroaches are the same; anything that is alive wishes to remain in existence. This is a very basic thing, existence, or the feeling 'I want to be'. This 'i' identifies with the body and the next thing that it wants is to be bigger. Swami Niranjanananda has expressed this idea beautifully in one of his Yoga Drishti series of books titled *Head, Heart and Hands*: "Since 'I exist', all the attributes of 'my' ahamkara are based on the instinct of survival. The awareness that 'I exist' as a person, as a being, is the identity of ahamkara. All the expressions of ahamkara are orientated and geared for self-preservation in the form of instinct."

Levels of consciousness

We have three main states: conscious, subconscious and unconscious, and then there is a fourth: the superconscious or *turiya*. The unconscious state is difficult to access. It is difficult to access even when we are knocked out and get a free ticket to unconsciousness. When the boxer gets into the ring and gets knocked out, is flat on the canvas in the boxing ring and out for the count of ten, he is unconscious. A few times in my life I have been knocked unconscious. I ran into a brick wall once, ran into a bus once, different things. My unconscious experiences have been nothing, absolutely nothing. Many people have had unconscious experiences. For example, Australia's richest man died in the 1990s. Newspaper reports said that he suffered a major heart attack on the polo field and was clinically dead for eight minutes until emergency medical officers revived him with electric shock treatment. Afterwards he said, "The good news is there's no devil. The bad news is there's no heaven. There's nothing." Yet others who are revived from death report wonderful experiences of light, wisdom and beings. Therefore, the awareness of people varies in both the unconscious state and beyond. Some can be aware, while others are not sufficiently refined to be able to see. Just as only some people are moved by beautiful poetry while all feel the rhythm of solid rock music.

Extensive psychological research has explored this subject of unconscious life after death. While it has its detractors, there is a powerful body of scientific documentation regarding after-death experiences, also known as near-death experiences by clinical researchers. This existence is in the realm of the unconscious, and we can experience it. Peter Fenwick is one such person who has studied these experiences. He is a neuropsychiatrist at the Institute of Psychiatry and he has been studying near-death experiences for over twenty years. He is one of the growing numbers of researchers who attest to an existence beyond the realms of the conscious and the dream state existence.

The unconscious contains the cause of all our activities. There is something in the unconscious state: all of our samskaras, all of our mental impressions and all of our karmas are there. The personal karmas driving us at the moment have something to do with the guru, kundalini and our *sadhana*, spiritual practice or discipline. What about the other karmas that we don't know about? There are many, many karmas in there which are deep in the unconscious; they are driving us, and when they come up there is no denying a powerful karma. There are weak karmas and there are strong karmas. Some karmas are very weak and we can do without or we can delay for a while. Others just happen and they can overwhelm us. Maybe you think you are going to live where you are for the rest of your life, then circumstances come up that force you to change plans and move into a completely different pursuit and circumstance. You have fixed that firm decision and one day something comes along rather suddenly and you've got a ticket to somewhere and you are somewhere else. Circumstances change and they are beyond your control.

According to yoga and karma, you have established these influences previously and the timing is not in the conscious logical realm. You have no control over the issue. For example, it may happen that you are determined never to come to an ashram. Suddenly, here you are, sitting in the ashram. It is the force of karma, the force of the unconscious. The unconscious is a very dynamic place and when this unconscious starts to unfold, we become very confused, because it is not what we planned. It is not what we thought about; it is all new. Normally, we are not sitting in the backroom of our mind. Suddenly, we've managed to open the door and have a look in and, oh my God, we want to shut the door again! It's got a strong spring on it, however. In order to cope in our day-to-day life, we need to relate normally. We need some physical activities to extrovert the consciousness, simple non-spicy food; we need to stimulate interest in ordinary social and political events. Then the mind comes out of haunting images and traumas within the unconscious and life begins to quieten. Therefore, we have to be very careful with our sadhana, particularly with swadhisthana. We have to walk through swadhisthana and the unconscious experiences of swadhisthana very slowly. We are actually students of swadhisthana and its consciousness and progress must be moderated so that with each exposure to new unconscious matter there is acceptance and no adverse reaction.

Temptation, another obstacle
Temptation has been mentioned previously. The media of the West, and now India, is full of tempting images. Today we live with the sensual images of celebrities all around us.

Many people having these sensual images can't do anything of note; some can sing and dance and some can't, however, they do attract attention and from that alone they succeed in their pursuit of wealth and fame. To us they are just an image, they are just a look. Yet, somehow they've got a lot of money and they are celebrities. For us students of the unconscious, they are wonderful examples that give us the opportunity to see how desires and drives are triggered by images and stimulated by the content of our own mind. We can see the essence of the matter, the mindstuff, and then realize that the image to which we are attracted is in our own mind, it is our own sensuality that relates in no way to the person in front of our eyes. Recall the story shared earlier from Swami Satyananda in *Kundalini Tanta*, of how the swami, trapped in swadhisthana, began to desire Mother Parvati when she manifested to him wearing almost transparent clothing until he realized that he was having the vision of a divine goddess, and prayed to his guru for help. This is the predicament of ordinary men.

The female experience is somewhat different, I am told. The female karma is that she wants to be wanted, and she wants to be wanted exclusively by her admirer. This is her limitation, so for Ma Kundalini to pass through swadhisthana she must transcend her need for God to want her and find her attractive. This swadhisthana female want will always be there at every stage of her evolution and right through life. This is the basis for women to wear perfume, jewellery and attractive clothes; it is a female characteristic and it is a limitation so long as it is a necessity.

5

The Six-Petalled Lotus

The experience of swadhisthana chakra is as a six-petalled lotus flower. Everyone has a six-petalled lotus flower in swadhisthana, and this is unanimously declared by such works as the tantras, Vedas, and Puranas, *Kundalini Tantra* by Swami Satyananda, *Satchakra Nirupanam*, as translated in *The Serpent Power* by Sir John Woodroffe, and *Laya Yoga* by Shyam Sundar Goswami; there is agreement in all reputed, reliable and respected texts about the petals and the *aksharas*, letters, on the petals. This leads us to conclude that this is spiritual testimony. These are all separate sources, independently written; they have not copied from each other. The ancient scriptures were not put into written form until about two thousand years ago; however, scholars write that the original records of yantras and mantras on cave walls look to be up to twenty thousand years old. All texts declare that swadhisthana has six petals, upon which the aksharas and the mantras, बं (*Bam*); भं (*Bham*); मं (*Mam*); यं (*Yam*); रं (*Ram*); and लं (*Lam*) are written.

Sanskrit as a revealed language
Why do the mantras appear on the petals? Where do they come from? Even people from other cultures, who use different characters for their alphabets, have the same Devanagari aksharas appear on the petals. Many thousands of years ago, when the great masters meditated on the lotus

flowers, they saw that there are four petals in mooladhara, six in swadhisthana, ten in manipura, twelve in anahata, sixteen in vishuddhi and two in ajna, making a total of fifty, which comprises the whole Devanagari alphabet. They saw all these letters and when they concentrated on the petals, they heard the sounds. From the sounds of the petals and aksharas on them came the Sanskrit language.

Those flower petals, created with the flow of prana, gave a wonderful vision inside the body of different colours with the aksharas shining like lightning; the colour of lightning onto the different coloured petals. Those petals that vibrated with that sound also gave a script, and this is the source of Sanskrit language. This is the source of Sanskrit sounds. When we start chanting Sanskrit, we experience a higher energetic state, the result of an increased flow of pranic energy and the resonance of the petals vibrating in harmony with the chanting. There is some inner vibration. *Prana* is the life force. Without prana, we're finished. When the prana is gone, we have death, *prana nidhana*. Not when the brain stops, not when the heart stops, the heart can stop, the brain can stop, but prana can't. When prana goes, we are dead.

While other languages have evolved over the centuries, Sanskrit was given from within. Sanskrit language has its origins in these revelations. It is not a created language, it is a revealed language; a language which came from within, and it has its source in the petals of the chakras.

Power of mantra

Many years ago in 1970, I took part in a three-year sannyasa training course in Munger, India. For one month the plan was to break the limitation of sleep by chanting the Vedas all night. While we were chanting it was easy to stay awake, yet when daytime came, especially after lunch and doing ordinary daytime duties such as cleaning and carrying and doing ordinary things, it was difficult. One day after lunch, after about two weeks of this sadhana, I could not keep my eyes open. The desire for sleep was overwhelming. Just then

Swami Satyananda called me and gave me the *Bhagavad Gita* to chant aloud. I had to sit outside his room and chant for one hour. After that chanting I was fully awake, alert and the sleepiness had gone. To this day, I am always impressed at the efficacy of Sanskrit chanting for raising the level of energy and wellbeing.

Here's another example of the power of Sanskrit mantras. Around 1900, an Englishman named Sir John Woodroffe was serving as Chief Justice of the Kolkata High Court. Sir John was a distinguished and very competent judge, capable of following cases closely and giving reasonable and rational judgements. His stenographer said to him one day, "Sir, please forgive me, but you've heard the evidence, and it's all recorded here, yet you've given the judgement in favour of those giving faulty evidence." After noting that his mistakes in handing down judgements were happening repeatedly, he looked at his mind and thought that something was very strange. He noticed that his mind was being swayed from one party to another. Even during a single civil case he would often find his mind being swayed between two parties; sometimes to one party and at other times biased towards the other party. Sir John made some enquiries, and he found out that both sides were using mantras with tantric *pandits*, priests, who were expert at winning court cases by biasing or influencing the mind of the judge. Sir John said, "That's astounding. Here I am, a High Court Chief Justice, and I'm getting swayed by these raggedy people who sit down there and chant mantras!" Sometimes they would just sit in the courtroom like disinterested, half-asleep visitors who were just hanging around. He became completely fascinated. He must have had spiritual karma, because he quit his job and decided to explore this aspect.

Sir John, with the help of a small crew of tantric or Sanskrit scholars, went to Assam, India, and they began to study the purer aspects of tantra. He did wonderful work and produced many good books, one of them being *Serpent Power*, which is a translation and commentary of the scriptural text *Sat Chakra Nirupanam,* meaning 'clarification on the six chakras'. It was written about six or seven hundred years ago by a great master, Swami Poornananda of Bengal, India. He wrote, in very concise and poetic Sanskrit, on the six chakras and the detailed experiences related to each of the six chakras.

Sir John translated, with full commentary, on every tiny little thing: the comments and the translations, the possibilities of the meaning, and so on. Eventually he returned to England. World War I had begun, however, so he was unable to publish his work. Once the war was over it was published, and many Indians, as well as the West, got to know about kundalini yoga. Until then, it was more or less a secret.

Thus, we are very grateful, first to Swami Poornananda for having written *Sat Chakra Nirupanam,* and second, to Sir John Woodroffe. He didn't write as Sir John Woodroffe; he didn't want to be persecuted by his own kind so he used a nom de plume, Arthur Avalon. Currently, kundalini and tantra have become mainstream and this story of Sir John Woodroffe has become part of history.

6

Vrittis Related to Swadhisthana

Sat Chakra Nirupanam describes the experience within the chakra: "Seated on the crocodile is the bija mantra *Vam*, stainless and white." These visions are real and they are replicated by many sadhakas. It's not just visualization in a meditation or yoga nidra class where students are instructed to 'see a temple bell, see the symbol *Om*, see a candle', and everybody sees a different candle. Rather, we are seeing the actual formation of our psychic personality as formed by our pranas. This is our pranic physiology. Just as we see that everyone has two arms and two eyes, in the same way, we have a six-petalled chakra in swadhisthana, with a moon, with a crocodile or *makara,* and with a mantra वं (*Vam*). It is depicted as a six-petalled lotus whose petals are connected with the six afflictive emotions: lust, anger, greed, delusion, pride and envy. When we concentrate on the petals, on those vibrating petals, we catch different moods. They're called *vrittis* or mental patterns of consciousness. Different patterns of consciousness are characterized in the petals, and we can experience those in meditation. Vrittis arise from the ego sense, *ahamkara,* which can be overcome by contemplating this chakra. The vrittis vary from sadhaka to sadhaka, from tantra to tantra. It doesn't matter really in the grand scheme of things. Ultimately, we have to be able to accept and realize what our vrittis are, in order to be able to transcend them. It is significant that lust is not emphasized as being the only vritti of swadhisthana, which is so often touted by modern commentators as the sex chakra.

There is some disagreement between the different chakra experiences of the moods or the vrittis, the impressions or the vibrations of each petal. This is shown in the table below. The *Rudra Yamala* and the *Adhyatma Viveka* are two separate summaries by reputed masters of the time. *Adhyatma Viveka* is taken from the study by Shyam Sundar Goswami in *Laya Yoga*. Susan Shumsky's book, *Exploring the Chakras*, has also been used as a reputable resource on the subject of chakras.

Petal No.	Adhyatma Viveka	Rudra Yamala	Shumsky
1	Affection or Indulgence	Lust, *kama*	Indulgence
2	Pitilessness	Anger, *krodha*	Pitilessness
3	Feeling of All Destructiveness	Greed, *lobha*	Feeling of All Destructiveness
4	Delusion	Delusion, *moha*	Delusion
5	Disdain	Pride, *mada*	Disdain
6	Suspicion	Envy, *matsarya*	Suspicion

Discovering vrittis while meditating on the individual petals begs the question, "Why do we have vrittis on our petals anyway?" The petals are connected with nadis, which in turn are connected through a psychic current to the brain, the organ of the mind. There's a direct connection between swadhisthana and the brain. This also tells us something: the six petals, with their six vrittis that we all suffer from; lust, pitilessness, feeling of all-destructiveness, delusion, disdain and suspicion; are more or less common to everyone. In Sage Patanjali's *Yoga Sutras* (1:2), it is stated: *Yogaschitta vritti nirodhah*. This means that ultimately, we have to stop all the vrittis. However, at this point we are becoming aware of the vrittis and attempting to accept and live with the vrittis.

Affection and indulgence

I know a wonderful swami who practised kriya yoga under Swami Satyananda's instruction years ago; she spent many hours performing sadhana. She used to work very hard, doing karma yoga as well as her many hours of sadhana. He would give her so much work, typing work and teaching and administrative work, that she would work until midnight or one o'clock in the morning, and then she was under the instruction, "Keep practising kriya yoga", which took her about two hours, and she'd get to sleep at about three o'clock in the morning. She would get up around half past three, and again, she would start. In this way, she went on for months and months.

One day, something suddenly changed in her, and she could hardly stand up, she was a bit vague and acted strangely. Swami Satyananda said, "Quick, we have to help her", so we had to help her walk, we had to help her move around, and slowly she came back. She had undergone a very deep spiritual experience. After she was coming back into normal consciousness and could speak again, she said to me, "Nityabodh, I'm having a very strange experience. I can see people the way I used to see them, and now suddenly I can see them as they truly are, without my old suspicions and conceptions. I can see the old conceptions just drift away and the new ones are here, and I think I'm having an anahata awakening, a psychic heart centre awakening." I said, "That's wonderful." She was gorgeous. When she said, "I think I've had an anahata awakening", it was so wonderful and inspiring.

This swami had a beautiful daughter who used to live in the ashram also. The daughter ran away to Holland and started doing exotic dancing or something similar. Her mother thought, 'My God, what's happened to my daughter?' The mother and daughter relationship was extremely strong. There was such affection between the two that even though she had just gone through a fantastic change due to her recent spiritual experience, even though she loved Swami Satyananda so much and the whole mission and the work, when her daughter was going down the wrong path, she just gave it all up and went back and tried to rescue her daughter.

I don't know the rest of the story, as I haven't heard anything since. This story demonstrates, however, the power of a vritti, which in this case was that of affection or indulgence. She didn't do anything wrong, a mother must care for her daughter, every civilized person would agree, and having a daughter is a lifelong karma, a lifelong duty. She had that karma to do. That karma was her residual vritti. Nobody really understands karma, but we can presume. We can presume that the mother in this story would have gone back to rescue her daughter and we can presume it was in vain, because everyone follows their own karmas. Thus she could be mourning, plunging herself back into worldly affairs and determined that in the next life she will avoid this problem by not having children. The vritti of affection or indulgence will still remain, however. It could express itself through service to other's children which is not binding and then in the next life, she could pursue spiritual goals without having to tear herself away.

Pitilessness

The next vritti is pitilessness, a kind of dismissiveness towards a person in difficulty. This dismissiveness comes as a protection of our own existence; usually it involves the giving out of money, time or effort. When you walk past beggars and the little kids say, "Give me rupees, give me rupees!" Poor little kids, but how do you deal with it? Do we deal with it in a pitiless way, "Nuisance, boy, I'm not giving you any money!" and dismiss them with a show of anger? You just don't bother to have pity. Why do we have to be pitiless? There are so many who are needy and definitely we cannot help all of them, and if we help one at random, hundreds more come and mob you. Maybe we haven't got any money. If at least we can want to help, even if we wish we could help, at least it would help us transcend our limitation of pitilessness.

Pitilessness is a vritti we may have, and we have to learn to deal with it so that it is not a bind. In order to become liberated so that divinity and enormous energy shine in every aspect of life, kundalini shakti must be able to ascend and not be limited by the demands of ahamkara. Ultimately, kundalini shakti must rise up from mooladhara and pass through each chakra, meeting all the vrittis within each chakra along the way. In mooladhara we are only dealing with four. That's easy, because they are not difficult vrittis. However, the next vrittis, meaning those in swadhisthana, are very difficult. Once this is crossed we come to the psychic difficulties, the psychic vrittis, and so on until all the chakras are crossed. In this manner, kundalini shakti moves up through the chakras, finally uniting with Shiva in sahasrara where their marriage occurs. Shiva and Shakti descend once again and then we have divinity established in our life. The whole problem, from the perspective of tantra, is that we have identified too completely with the material. We have taken the divinity out of the material. We are then only left with the 'stuff'. We ask, "Where's the God in this thing? Where's the God in that thing? Where's the God in him or her?" However, for some devoted people who have awakened divinity, God is everywhere and in everything.

Destructiveness

Feelings of all-destructiveness are more difficult to understand. There is nothing gained in destruction, so a logical approach will not give us an understanding. Indeed, in our own lives we create something, then we build on the creation so that we become comfortably established, and then we do something almost by accident to destroy everything we have established. It certainly is a limitation of our mind and blocks any expansion of consciousness; it is destructive materially and spiritually. Therefore we must continue to build in spite of our urges to destroy.

Delusion and disdain

Delusion is a kind of tamasic state of comfort. Clarity is the state we must always strive for. Disdain is our vain attempt to promote ourselves to a higher status in life not by our effort, but by looking for those we can categorize as less important than ourselves.

Once again, in kundalini yoga we have to purify the mind so that Shakti can ascend right up to sahasrara where Shiva and Shakti unite. After that highest of spiritual experiences, Shiva and Shakti both descend to bring divinity into every aspect of life.

Suspicion

Haven't you heard about the two psychiatrists? As they were walking past each other in the morning, one said to the other, "Good morning," and the other said, "Good morning," and they both went away thinking, 'What did he mean by that?' Suspicion is a potential character trait of humankind. It prevents us from unwarily falling into a trap. If we think there is something not right with a situation or there's something fishy going on, we are being suspicious and this is a quality of swadhisthana.

In uniting with the divine, many people are sceptical and suspicious, based on a lack of empirical evidence, and as a result, they cannot fully surrender. In order for Ma Kundalini to pass through swadhisthana, you must be able to leave behind suspicion when uniting with the divine and reapply it when you go to the market. It is what we do in the world, anyhow; when you go home to your loved ones you leave behind suspicion and analysis, but as soon as you step back into the world, you automatically put on your worldly psychological armour.

7

Image and Symbology

The *aksharas*, meaning the Sanskrit letters, are the colour of lightning, the petals are vermilion, and the pericarp is black. Pericarp is the term for the centre part of a flower where the seeds are held. This is the traditional view; it's not a universal view. Some people see swadhisthana with black or different colours of petals. Sometimes people see it as grey, and there are different reasons for the colours they see. Everybody tries to explain it and I have my own opinions also, but let's explore this a little. Tantra, and the concept of the goddess being implicit in every fragment of creation, is the basis of our collective knowledge as human beings. However, in our modern times, these ancient teachings have been manipulated to make kundalini yoga a marketable item. One result of this manipulation is the availability of thousands of books on this subject, and on tantra in general, making it very difficult to know which one to buy to get the proper traditional knowledge. You can't go through every one. Slowly we're sorting out the reputable sources.

This image of swadhisthana chakra is just a picture. Your experience of swadhisthana may not reflect that artist's experience or vision. Traditionally, the petal with the akshara बं (*Bam*) shown here to be the petal at twelve o'clock, is usually at one o'clock. The petals should be rotated to the right to reflect the traditional view. The image shows all six aksharas on the petals as well as the crescent moon, crocodile and the bija mantra वं (*Vam*), all of which will be explored and discussed.

The chakra diagram below is closer to the classical or traditional descriptions, with the first petal at one o'clock and having six outward facing petals. Inside the pericarp, we have two circles forming a crescent moon: a bigger circle and a smaller circle. The outer

An artist's impression of swadhisthana

circle, the bigger of the two, has petals facing out. This symbolizes the conscious dimension of our personality. This is our external consciousness. The smaller circle within it has petals facing in. If you look at the petals in one way, it appears as if the inner circle petals could be facing out, but they're not, they're facing in. The petals facing in represent the unconscious dimension. In-between the two circles is the white crescent moon, the form symbolizing the water element. It is a white moon. In the white moon is the white bija mantra, वं (*Vam*) sitting on the back of a white crocodile. Please use your imagination to make the crocodile white, the वं (*Vam*) white, and the crescent moon white. They can all be seen because each item in the chakra is progressively whiter and stands out in relief from the other.

Summarizing, we have a white moon. Sitting on the white moon, or in the white moon, is a white crocodile, and

Classical image of swadhisthana

47

sitting on the white crocodile is the bija mantra, वं (*Vam*). In this way, we have formed our swadhisthana yantra.

Pranas and differences in experience

The petal colours are traditionally vermilion, or bright red. However, Swami Satyananda writes, "It can be experienced as black." He says that swadhisthana is grey or black, yet throughout all the books it is traditionally bright red. It has been suggested by Goswami that the cause of the variations in the experience of colours is due to different pranas. There are five major pranas or divisions of pranic energy within the body: *prana*, which operates in the area of the heart and lungs; *apana*, which governs the lower abdominal region; *samana*, which is essential for digestion; *udana*, which primarily governs the extremities; *vyana*, the reserve of pranic energy which pervades the whole body. Goswami says that if the experience of swadhisthana is black, it means prana was flowing at the time and not apana.

The five pranas have different colours when they flow, and depending upon which prana is flowing predominantly, you will see that colour. I question whether this is a valid explanation, because none of the pranas are black. Therefore, the experience of black petals in swadhisthana does not relate to prana. Prana is not black. None of the pranas, whether prana, apana, samana, udana or vyana, is black. However, the guna tamas is experienced as black, and even if the seer has transcended the gunas, the *manomaya kosha*, the mental sheath, is still subject to the gunas and could explain the experience of black petals. The master who is experiencing the vision of a six-petalled black lotus flower will be able to see that tamasic state, as he is a *trigunatita*, someone who has transcended the three gunas. He is able to see from a higher state of consciousness, 'Aha, tamas is now flowing. Aha, rajas is now flowing. Aha, now the mind is in a balanced sattwic state and it is gold, it is made of gold petals.'

In this way, we can come to an understanding of the colour variation on the petals. On this point there is no published material, just the ideas of Shyam Sundar Goswami. Ancient texts mention petal colours such as vermilion red, fire-like red, lustrous red, whitish red, deep red, lightning-like and golden-coloured. Not everything is written about chakras, and we have to investigate them deeply in order to come to our own conclusions. We have to be able to have our own experiences and if we want to explain to the investigators of yogic lore, then we have to figure it out ourselves and have the means to explain the experience.

Makara or the crocodile, the unconscious

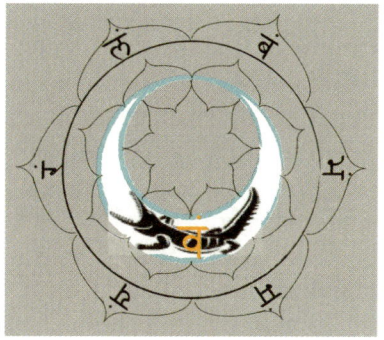

Inside the pericarp of swadhisthana

The animal in swadhisthana is the *makara*, which is similar to a crocodile and is the vehicle of Varuna, lord of the sea. The nature of the crocodile is well known. When we go to crocodile-infested areas we are very wary, because this animal is almost impossible to see. People standing by the riverbank are pulled in by its jaws and the unfortunate individual just disappears into the depths. The crocodile has survived since ancient times, where other species have become endangered or disappeared with the ravages of change. The crocodile has survived and continues to thrive wherever there is water, be it next to a metropolis or in remote regions. It just swims on the surface, with its two eyes and a little bit of its nose showing. If there's a crocodile hanging about in a nice pond of water, it could be mistaken for a piece of wood or a floating log; it's just there, it's so still. It's so quiet. The moment you put your leg or arm anywhere near it, however, it will become completely animated and leap up, grab you and take you down, which is the nature of the makara in us, our unconscious. You never see it again. It takes whatever it is down to the bottom of the lake. The makara, the crocodile, takes it down to the bottom of the water, eats and digests and then excretes there. The excrement of a crocodile is completely different to what he digested, and this is the same story with the formation of our unconscious karmas and samskaras.

Earlier in this book, I mentioned the story of police throwing guns into the river to hide incriminating evidence, and when the guns were pulled out, they were almost unrecognizable as guns. In the same way, if, when you were a little child, something happened, maybe some tiny thing: somebody yelled at you, somebody looked at you rather sternly or with a controlling frown, because you could not fully understand, you told yourself, 'I don't even want to think about it.' Children shrink from everything that's negative as they cannot analyze it. The experience goes down with their crocodile into the water. This idea of water and crocodile is not foreign to the mind.

This is not empty symbology. The symbolic crocodile typifies the nature of our psychology. Below is some classical psychology from *Psychology Themes and Variations* by Wayne Weiten. This section has been included because it demonstrates how psychology is limited to coping mechanisms, whereas yoga is determined to stimulate the unconscious and purify it of suppressed events from the past or symbolically release it from the jaws of the crocodile.

- Psychology is theoretically diverse. It evolves along a socio-historical context and is empirical. Its intellectual parents were 19th century philosophy and physiology, which shared an interest in the mysteries of the mind.
- Freud was the first psychologist to acknowledge the unconscious thoughts that influence one's behaviour. He defined three levels of awareness: conscious awareness, preconscious, which is just below the surface of awareness, and the unconscious. He also defined the id as 'primitive, instinctive, acts on pleasure principle, wants immediate gratification, illogical, irrational, fantasy-oriented'. He defined the ego as 'decision making, reality principle,

delayed gratification, mediates between id and external social world'; and the superego as 'the moral component, social standards, what is right and wrong'. These three are in constant conflict, causing anxiety which triggers defence mechanisms such as:
- *Repression*: Keeping distressing thoughts and feelings buried in the unconscious
- *Projection*: Attributing one's own thoughts and feelings to another
- *Displacement*: Diverting emotional feelings, usually anger, from their original source to a substitute target
- *Reaction formation*: Behaving in a way that is exactly opposite to one's true feelings
- *Regression*: A reversion to immature patterns of behaviour
- *Rationalization*: Creating false, but plausible excuses to justify unacceptable behaviour
- *Identification*: Bolstering self-esteem by forming an imaginary or real alliance with some person or group.
- Jung was Freud's student who furthered his work and suggested a collective unconscious. The personal unconscious houses material not within the person's consciousness because it's been repressed or forgotten.
- According to Jung, the collective unconscious is a storehouse of latent memory traces inherited from our ancestral past. Each person shares the collective unconscious with the entire human race. It contains 'the whole spiritual heritage of mankind's evolution, born anew in the brain structure of every individual'. Archetypes are emotionally-charged images, for example, mandalas from different cultures are evidence of collective unconscious because they have universal meaning. Some psychologists hold that the image of 'the still lake' is an archetypal image and could be included in Jungian psychology.
- Jung was also the first psychologist to describe introversion and extroversion.

- Adler was a member of Freud's psychoanalytic society and like Jung, he diverted from Freud, believing an individual's drive was for superiority and the individual would strive to adapt and improve and master life's challenges. People strive for superiority to compensate for feelings of inferiority, often by overcompensating.
- The 1990s saw evolutionary psychology emerge. It suggests that patterns of behaviour seen in a species are evolutionary, just like anatomical characteristics. This reasoning suggests that natural selection favours behaviours which enhance an organism's reproductive success.
- Humanism is a theoretical orientation that emphasizes the unique qualities of humans, especially their freedom and potential for growth.
- Abraham Maslow's theory of self-actualization and hierarchy of needs suggests basic needs must be met before less basic needs are aroused. At the top of the hierarchy is the need for self-actualization.

Psychologists have revealed and described a multitude of mechanisms and perspectives that we adopt to cope with our earthly suffering mind and body. The very discipline of psychology, itself questioning, researching, measuring and categorizing the mind, brain and behaviour, can be considered a mechanism in itself. However, the path to liberation from the unconscious patterns is not explored in psychology. While defence mechanisms are often thought of as negative reactions, some of these defences can be helpful. For example, utilizing humour to overcome a stressful, anxiety-provoking situation can actually be an adaptive defence mechanism.

Moon as a symbol of the mind
The crescent moon shape is formed by two non-concentric circles, one bigger than the other. The sun and moon are the two most powerful forces in worldly life. The sun is masculine and represents our external or extroverted personality. The

moon is feminine and symbolizes our internal or introverted personality. In yoga, the subtle equivalents of our sympathetic and parasympathetic nervous systems are named *pingala* and *ida*, symbolized traditionally by the sun and moon and reflecting our external and internal personalities. The relationship between the moon and our states of mind is well known, and the highly charged emotional states experienced during the full moon, and the thirteenth day of each fortnight after both the full moon and the new moon, are often volatile times. There is a lake in Tibet near Mount Kailash called *Mansarovar*, meaning 'lake of the mind'. It is famed for being very still and quiet and just to be there gives memorable peace to the whole being. Indeed, many who have returned from visiting the 'lake of the mind' talk of deep and divine experiences usually attained only after years of meditation. There is a link between water, the mind and the moon. The mind is a lake or an ocean. The mind is water, symbolized by the crescent moon, therefore the moon is the symbol for the mind in the tranquil lake in the swadhisthana yantra. It is a lotus pond or a lake.

The mind is not confined to the head. Our thoughts are there and the physical brain is too, yet there is a lot more. The mind envelopes the whole physical body and it is very subtle. It is known in yoga as *manomaya kosha*, one of the five sheaths or *koshas* which cover the self, and specifically it is the mental sheath. The unconscious aspects of the mind manifest in every part of our being. Sadness or loneliness is located in the heart, envy and jealousy are located in the stomach, lust can overwhelm most of the body and these feelings come from the unconscious mind. To face the unconscious and accept its contents is to open the path for kundalini to pass through svadhisthana at the base of the spine. Crossing this ocean of the mind is such an enormous task that we appeal to our guru for his compassion to help us across, as in the hymn *Sadguru Vandana*, which opens with the line *Bhava sagara tarana karana he* – "Please, take this poor soul across to the other side of the ocean of mind. Have compassion on this poor lost soul." We have to cross the ocean of the mind to the other side, and so we ask our guru for assistance. We have to cross this ocean and see everything along the way.

Bija mantra of swadhisthana

In the centre of the pericarp, on the back of the makara is the *bija mantra* or seed mantra, वं (*Vam*). Each chakra has a bija mantra. This seed mantra is the beginning of the spiritual aspect; it is the doorway to the deities within the chakras. The seed mantra वं (*Vam*) is to be repeated as a sadhana. In order to purify the chakra, in order to purify the mind and bring out the qualities, we repeat the mantras on the petals. In order to go deeper and deeper into the chakra, we repeat the bija mantra and we visualize the bija mantra, because the bija mantra transforms into the deity Varuna. By visualizing the seed mantra वं, you are visualizing the form which transforms into the deity Varuna.

Varuna

Sat Chakra Nirupanam states: "Within swadhisthana is the white, shining, watery region of Varuna, of the shape of the half moon, and therein seated on a makara, is the bija वं (*Vam*), stainless and white as the autumnal moon."

Shyam Sundar Goswami in *Laya Yoga* quotes a number of diverse texts (which can be referenced in order of appearance at the back of this book) and finds agreement within the following descriptions of Varuna:

"In the pericarp of swadhisthana is situated Varuna."

"The watery Varuna bija is within this chakra."

"The Varuna bija which is within the Varuna region has four arms and is seated on a makara."

"The Varuna bija has a *pasha*, noose, in his hand."

"A semi-lunar water region is within the pericarp of swadhisthana."

"The 'water region' is half-moon shaped and white and encloses the bija वं (*Vam*)."

Goswami also writes in *Laya Yoga*: "The bija aspect वं (*Vam*) is the deity Varuna. From the bija व (*Va*) arises Varuna. There is no difference between the bija and the form. Varuna is in the form of वं as well as a divine form."

Vedic literature tells us of Varuna's role in the world, and from these references we can infer the connection between the worldly or exoteric role and the microcosmic function of Varuna within the unconscious. The study below is by Erica Goy (April 2008).

Varuna's place in swadhisthana

According to Usha Choudhuri's text *Indra and Varuna in Indian Mythology*, Varuna is considered one of the oldest gods in Hindu mythology and is noted as a 'universal monarch'. In the past, Varuna was said to be king of the gods, holding utmost power in vedic India. Scholars such as J. Hakin and others suggest in his book *Asiatic Mythology: A Detailed Description and Explanation of the Mythologies of All the Great Nations of Asia* that Varuna is a 'majestic Jehovah, preserver of eternal order and redresser of wrongs'. Varuna himself is related to the skies and water, controlling the cosmic order. Though there are only roughly twelve hymns dedicated to him in the *Rig Veda*, Varuna is still in charge of many things and has many obligations as a vedic god.

Creator and preserver of heaven and earth: Varuna is god of the sky and the water and the celestial ocean, as well as lord of law and of the underworld. He is a prominent deva in the *Rig Veda* and lord of the heavens and the earth. Varuna's main obligations involve both creating and preserving the heaven and earth and protecting the waters, including all oceans and rivers, celestial and terrestrial.

He is to stay strong to the *rita*, the keeping of cosmic order. His duties include commanding the darkness of the night and keeping a separation between night and day. The sky blankets Varuna. Regarding Varuna, Hakins' text also states: "He knows not sleep, and nothing escapes his vigilance, for the stars, his eyes, are without number." Choudhuri credits Varuna with the creation of the rivers and maintenance of the volume of their waters so that they do not overflow, and he continues to watch over water in its entirety, and also states: "The duties of this majestic deity are to make the stars come out at night and magically, Varuna's powers cause the stars to disappear during the day." According to the same author, he holds the task of keeping earth in its full form, and being an omniscient vedic god, Varuna 'knows the path of the birds flying through the air. He, abiding in the ocean, knows also the course of the ships'.

Symbology of Varuna: Though Varuna is rarely depicted, if one is to look hard enough, images are profuse. Varuna is depicted as a fierce white god with perfect posture, riding upon a marine monster known as a makara. The makara, though commonly accepted as the crocodile as mentioned earlier, is still not fully understood. Some believe it to have originally been a dolphin-like creature, seeming to be half-crocodile. Others believe it to have the legs of an antelope and the tail of a fish. According to the Vedas, Varuna is said to have four faces, one closely resembling the features of Agni, the god of fire. He has many arms of grace and a noose. Varuna's noose is made from a snake and is grasped in his right hand, accompanied by a shining gold foot. He wears a short, floating, sleeveless cloak of gold colouring and complete golden armour. As mentioned in another text by W.J. Wilkins, Varuna lives in a house of one thousand doors, thus being constantly attainable to humankind. Choudhuri also believes that Varuna's palace is one of a thousand gates, where he resides inside upon his golden throne. Varuna's palace has multiple doors to symbolize and represent his uninterrupted movement and knowledge.

Varuna's connection to the water element: Vedic history explores the idea that Varuna is not solely affiliated with just water itself, but according to Hajime Nakamura in his text, he is affiliated with both 'the water elements of ether and earth'. Many profound scholars like Georges Dumezil believe Varuna to be connected to many different ideas and concepts. Dumezil believes there to be a link between Mitra, the god of oath, and Varuna. In his essay on Mitra and Varuna, Dumezil interprets *mitra* as friend and links Varuna's name to the root *var,* which means 'to bind'. Wilkins states that Mitra and Varuna come together as one in many hymns and are written about quite often, and Varuna is occasionally solo in other hymns. According to Dumezil, each time Mitra is mentioned in a vedic hymn, Varuna is also elevated. Choudhuri states that both Mitra and Varuna are considered to be great gods, in control of the seas and rivers, and associated closely with each other in the *Atharva Veda*. Thus, Varuna is closely associated with Mitra, accompanying Mitra as a divine king. Choudhuri states Varuna to be 'the ruler of gods, along with all men' expressing both 'physical and moral demands'.

Myths maintain that Varuna became a powerful vedic god through Indra, the god of war and weather. Wilkins presents the myth of a demon stealing the entirety of the universe's water, which created a large conflict amongst the heavens and the earth. It was not Varuna alone who fought off the demon, rather he fought alongside Indra. Nakamura states that 'due to this, Indra was able to supplant the lordship of Varuna and become lord of the gods himself', taking the ultimate power from Varuna. Yet Varuna still remains a part of the Hindu culture. Though Varuna still holds power, as a god he is not nearly as important as he once was. This being the case, Varuna is not widely worshipped by many, but still plays an important role in the lives of some. In particular, Varuna is highly worshipped by people about to embark on long sea voyages as well as fishermen before they set out to sea. They pray to Varuna for help so that they can be guided and find the right path and avoid typhoons and all the rest. He is worshipped by farmers during the long, hot, dry seasons of drought. Hakin states that Varuna is also worshipped by those who fear him, mostly in an attempt to free themselves of their sins and wrongdoings, and along the same lines Choudhuri presents that Varuna liberates us of all sin: "Keep far from us the evil, *nirrti,* with unfriendly looks, and liberate us from whatever sins we may have committed."

God of justice and punishment: Varuna is said to be the vedic god of punishment. Varuna is obligated to stay strong and keep the cosmic order; he holds the order of the skies and waters. Of all Hindu deities, Varuna is the judgemental god, providing justice and punishment to everyone. He is the law holder and watches over all through the sun and the stars. The sky blankets Varuna and he keeps watch on all of us through the stars. The stars are his informers. All those stars out there tell him what's going on, what we're doing and he keeps tabs on them. Now this is the external aspect; however, the internal aspect is also there.

In the book, *Indra and Varuna in Indian Mythology,* Choudhuri states: "Varuna removes the bad elements of yajna and protects its virtuous elements. Varuna is vigilant over *satya,* truth, and *anrita,* falsehood." Therefore, being true he does not allow people to disobey the universal law and is extremely vigilant regarding people's sins. When a sin is committed, Varuna sees all and hears all, and those people are punished rigorously. Many human beings fear Varuna as he is in charge of the moral actions and the thoughts of all people. Dumezil states: "Varuna is the sovereign under his attacking aspect, dark, inspired, violent, terrible, warlike." Varuna is a protector of the good and punisher of the evil, and he cannot be fooled by anyone. Varuna is said to be able to extend the lives of the good and shorten the lives of the sinners. Regarding this, Choudhuri interprets the use of Varuna's noose as being 'characterized with the power of seizing and trying foes, the demons, and the sinners'. When Varuna confronts a sinner, bargains are made and contracts are enforced; he lassoes them with his noose as they plead for forgiveness and mercy. Although Varuna is only a judgemental deity, if he so chooses, Varuna is able to share the obligations of Yama, the god of death. As posed by Wilkins, of all the vedic gods, Varuna has the highest of moral character, and is called upon in the notion of purity.

Like many other vedic gods, Varuna is accompanied by a wife, Varuni. Though little is written by scholars about Varuni, westerners believe her to be the goddess of wine. Wilkins presents that Varuni, coexisting with Varuna, sits on a throne scattered with diamonds amongst other gods and goddesses present in Varuna's court, such as Samudra, lord of the seas, Ganga, goddess of the Ganges and other gods and goddesses of springs, rivers and lakes. To this day, even though Varuna is not as powerful as he once was, he still plays an important role in Indian lives. It is Varuna who expresses his power through his actions and through his obligations as a vedic deity. Being an omniscient god, Varuna has unlimited control over the Hindu people, and every action is judged by Varuna himself. Perhaps the most significant reason behind Varuna's popularity is judgement. Varuna appears to play a powerful role in the lives of sinners, and under a strict sense of duty, he rids the Indian society of sins and wrongdoings. Though Varuna is not widely worshipped, he is nevertheless a powerful and important deity in Indian culture and tradition.

This esoteric interpretation of Varuna clarifies the role of Varuna within us. To the unawakened mind, the unconscious is unknown, yet the deity Varuna never sleeps and remains always watchful. He is the moral force within us, often forcing us into denial because we cannot face our own moralistic Varuna nature. With each and every paragraph we can draw an esoteric interpretation.

God is in my swadhisthana: You may ask, "What is a form of God doing in my swadhisthana?" Monotheistic philosophies hold that God has no body, so we cannot have a god of any part of the body. However, tantra stems from the philosophy that the divine is not limited to a formless, invisible existence, but comes to exist in the manifest dimension through the process of creation. Unfortunately, in our worldly pursuits we have identified with the material objects and forgotten about the divine in them, possibly because it seems very unlikely that the same form and quality of God that created the universe lives in a blade of grass or in swadhisthana chakra.

To ease the transition of accepting both the unseen God in heaven and God in a blade of grass or a chakra, tantra offers an explanation of how this may come to be in its concept of creation. According to this concept, before creation there was nothing but Shiva and Shakti; Shakti being pure cosmic energy and Shiva being pure consciousness. This pure consciousness was formless and beyond definition, yet it already contained within itself everything, every being, and all knowledge, like a blueprint. All that it required was Shakti to manifest all this knowledge lying formless within it. They separated, and through a sequential step-down process, creation occurred. Tantra says that since Shiva and Shakti, or God, created everything that exists, why not allow oneself to see their divinity in a blade of grass, a chakra, or even another human being? I am a sceptic by nature, but I have no problem accepting the experience of the deity Varuna, the experience that great masters have had over thousands of years and written about in the tantras, vedic shastras, Puranas, and in other texts.

There are deities in each aspect of life; however, we are not yet aware of them. Logic demands that deities do exist in manifest dimension. "What logic?" you may ask. Our qualities of consciousness as well as our manifest form of energy, the body, came from a source or a cause. "Nothing comes from nothing," say the Upanishads, therefore the seeds of our being must be in the Source. Furthermore, within the universe there is an order, and within the sushumna nadi there is an order or a structure. Even when things appear to be random, mathematicians find order within any random selection. From where does this design come? The original Source must have the ability and knowledge of planning systematic development. We all have the potential qualities of loving and caring; there is a unity in the grand plan and we are all attracted to it. This attraction manifests as the desire for spiritual life and it is the quality of loving compassion and devotion.

If within the grand plan there exists such an infinite diversity of varied and systematically designed organisms, surely two things are possible: firstly, for the organisms to be of the same spirit and energy from which they came, and secondly, that this spirit has a form. Why not? Are we, with our sceptical and limited knowledge, going to place the limitations of our formal and rational education upon a Supreme Consciousness or God, limiting this energy to either having a form, or not having one at all? Is that form visible only to those who have purified the mind to be able to see very fine vibrations? Lord Krishna settled this question once and for all in Chapter 12 of the *Bhagavad Gita*, when he declared that a manifest form of God and an unmanifest, formless God were both valid. Therefore, we have a response to that doubting intellect which may be sceptical at the mention of Varuna in swadhisthana or of God in any form.

In practice, we have to be able to visualize and concentrate on the form of Varuna in order to open greater depths of experience within this chakra. The form of Varuna on which to concentrate is white, having four arms and seated on a makara, a crocodile. He holds the *pasha*, noose made with a snake, in one of his hands.

Our inner judge: Varuna has the form, वं (*Vam*). Varuna is *Vam*, the bija mantra, and *Vam* is Varuna, the deity. There's not as much written about Varuna as there is for other gods; however, as mentioned earlier, what we do know is that he is the judge. From the external point of view, in the hymns of the Vedas, he's referred to as the judge, the person who keeps things in order. Just as astrological Saturn does not let us forget the karma in our chart, in the same way Varuna reminds us of the deeds and misdeeds we have performed, thus necessitating that we deal with it. He keeps constant watch over us. Scholars tell us that Varuna is a majestic Jehovah, the witness, the preserver of eternal order and redresser of wrongs.

We all have within us a judge. Is that surprising to you? Inside there is a judge which, if things are out of order, reminds you by telling you, "No, no, this is not right, what I'm doing is not right." Sometimes people say, "Oh no, he is wrong. I'm all right, but he's wrong." This is the extroverted judge that the ignorant use to avoid seeing their own personality. This characteristic is known as 'judgemental' and it divides the world into two: the part of the world that they approve of and the other part which they disapprove of. If you are on the receiving end of such a judgement, it is an uncomfortable position and if you yourself are the judge, your view is limited to what you approve of, and this narrowed perspective makes for a limited life.

The interesting thing about Varuna as the internal judge is that he is the one directing his steed, the makara, to take the experiences to the unconscious until we are mature enough to deal with them. He is an internal judge. We are constantly trying to improve our qualities and bring our personality into order so that it is balanced, and that's Varuna's job. As Varuna is the king of the sea, he has to take us across this ocean of consciousness and unconsciousness, karmas and samskaras.

Lust and sexuality as obstacles: In the images seen of Varuna, he is holding a noose made of a snake, which is very interesting. We now arrive at the interpretation of this noose, the snake. Where do we get 'hung up' while passing through swadhisthana? How do we hang or trap ourselves in the noose of the snake? Why a snake, why not a rope? It is because the snake symbolizes lust and sexuality, and the noose is the trap we get caught in. Once we are in it, it is a trap. Getting out of it is a struggle, at least that's my understanding. Varuna controls body fluids, sexual function, circulation, eggs and sperm; Varuna's noose is lust and sexuality, and it is also the trap of selfishness, 'my-ness' and 'I-ness'. These things that we have, these qualities or vrittis that we have on the petals of our chakras, they are our limitations. We trap ourselves in life; we are caught up by these qualities, by these psychological aspects which imprison us, and it's entirely of our own making. We can't go on blaming Varuna for it. He doesn't go running around on his crocodile with a lasso trying to trap us and pull us down. No, this is a noose of our own making. This is all of our own making. This entire psychology is not external; it's within all of us. If I have Varuna in my swadhisthana, then that's me. It's not something which I can simply deny or disown, no, it's me, a deeper part of myself, a very subtle part of myself. My quest then is to become liberated from these restrictions, symbolized by the noose, which I have placed on myself.

Lord Vishnu

When we concentrate on the bindu of *Vam*, or within the bindu, we get the experience of Lord Vishnu, who is also known as Hari. In *Sat Chakra Nirupanam* it is stated: "May Hari, who is within the bindu of Varuna, who is the pride of early youth, whose body is of a luminous blue, beautiful to behold, who is dressed in yellow raiment, is four-armed, wears the srivatsa and the Kaustubha, protect us!"

Lord Vishnu is the presiding deity of the chakra. Imagine the experience of being able to go into *Vam*, into the bindu above *Vam*, and experiencing the mantra as divine, then as Lord Varuna, and then manifesting in the lap of Varuna is the magnificence of Lord Vishnu. This experience is deep inside the pericarp, inside the bija mantra वं (*Vam*).

Vishnu

Symbology of Lord Vishnu: In the hands of Lord Vishnu are the conch, called *Panchajanyam*, the five layers of wisdom, as well as joy. The *sudarshan* or discus of Vishnu represents consciousness and when concentrating on the hub of the discus, vision of the supreme God arises. Sudarshan also means beautiful vision, correct vision or excellent darshan. On account of the excellent vision gained from concentration on the hub of the discus, it is given the appellation 'sudarshan'. Lord Vishnu also carries a mace or war-club called Kaumadi. The Puranas tell wonderful stories of evil being conquered and social order being restored through Kaumadi. Kaumadi is considered a source of happiness; the weapon destroys ignorance by imparting the spiritual knowledge contained within the fifty Sanskrit mantras vibrating on the fifty petals from mooladhara to ajna chakras. The fourth item Lord Vishnu holds in his hands is the lotus. This lotus is in full bloom, symbolizing supreme consciousness, and it is our heart lotus. Our *atman* or soul resides in this lotus of the heart. As is the case with all images of spiritual deities, each and every symbol carries a deep significance.

The beautiful dark-blue form of Lord Vishnu arises in the bindu of वं (*Vam*), seen sitting in the lap of Varuna. The *srivatsa* is a mark on his chest symbolizing Prakriti. On his chest is one of the celebrated gems, the *kaustubha*, obtained during the churning of the ocean by the gods and demons and symbolizing atman.

The ornaments of Lord Vishnu are a crown and armlets and Lord Vishnu wears makara or crocodile-shaped earrings. He also wears a mala of flowers around his neck. It is a multi-season garland. It never fades and it never dies. This enduring mala of flowers is said to represent Maya, the mother of the variegated universe of which we are a part. *Maya* means illusion or delusion, and when used in certain contexts, for example capitalized and given a personality, she is another form or power of Shakti, representing that power to delude, to cast a spell on and veil the truth from her created beings. Maya controls us, and Vishnu controls Maya; she is held passively around his neck as a garland of flowers. Although Maya controls all beings, she in turn is controlled by Lord Vishnu.

Rakini, the doorkeeper

Sat Chakra Nirupanam states (v. 17): "It is here that Rakini always dwells. She is the colour of a blue lotus. The beauty of her body is enhanced by her uplifted arms holding various weapons. She is dressed in celestial raiment and ornaments and her mind is exalted by the drinking of ambrosia."

Rakini shines in swadhisthana, and she is beautiful. Here the author writes 'dwells', whereas in the original text the word is *bhati,* meaning 'shines'. 'She is the colour of a blue lotus' is translated literally in the original text to say, "Her radiant beauty equals the interior of the blue lotus." In her uplifted arms she holds a spear, a lotus, a drum and an axe. In many scriptures the word 'ambrosia' refers to the nectar that drops from sahasrara. Here, the drinking of this nectar exalts and infuses Rakini with its divine energy.

She is revealed as one of the forms of kundalini herself by various scriptural texts. It is said, "Rakini is Kundali", which means she is one of the forms of kundalini shakti. Her darshan is the good omen that a kundalini experience is imminent. Therefore, Rakini is called the doorkeeper of swadhisthana.

Descriptions for Rakini are diverse. In his book *Laya Yoga*, Goswami describes the characteristics of Rakini and cites many texts as he does so. Goswami reports that in the *Kanakamalini Tantra* (5:23), Rakini is described as 'red in colour, two-armed and fawn-eyed and is shining with the vermilion mark on her forehead. Her eyes are gracefully painted with collyrium, she is dressed in white raiment and adorned with various ornaments, her face as beautiful as the moon'. In *Kularnava Tantra* (10:53), she is described thus: "Divine Rakini is dark-coloured or black and adorned with various ornaments and holds a sword and a shield." *Koulavalitantra* (22:80) affirms: "Rakini is dark blue or black and holds in her hands a spear or trident, the *vajra*, thunderbolt, a lotus and a drum." Kalicharana cites a verse stating, "Rakini is dark blue or black, holds in her hands a spear or trident, a lotus, a drum and a sharp chisel. She is powerful and has three red eyes and prominent teeth; the great lustrous, divine Rakini is seated on a double lotus." Kalicharana comments here that to see Rakini seated on a red lotus is to understand that all six Shaktis everywhere are also seated upon red lotuses. Another view is in the *Nirguna Brahma Swarupa*: "She is known as Rakini. She is mostly worshipped by the tantrics. She has a fearsome appearance and each of her four arms holds a different weapon of destruction. She is blue in colour with lustrous smooth skin and she has voracious drives of lust. She has three eyes, each bloodshot. She sometimes has been depicted with three faces controlling the past, present and future."

Rakini controls *bhuvah loka*, the intermediate realm between earth and heaven, as well as the nature of the person. This swadhisthana level of consciousness is intermediate. It is above earthly or material consciousness and it is below divine consciousness. All karmas of the person, every single activity done by the person is stored in the unconscious bhuvah loka which can be awakened or brought into conscious awareness through concentration on swadhisthana or on the aspects of divine Rakini.

There are multiple descriptions of the experiences of the shakti Rakini. It is also written that she has two heads, each with two eyes, and she is dark blue or vermilion in colour. She is very beautiful and sits on a double red lotus. She is shyamavarna. *Shyamavarna* means that in the heat of summer the body is always cool, and in the cold of winter the body is always warm, which is ideal. She is lustrous and she is the goddess of the vegetable kingdom. Therefore, it is said that it is very important to be a vegetarian to gain Rakini's favour in order to pass through and open the door to higher experience. Each of Rakini's four hands holds a symbolic article:

Trident: This is her goad to help us control the mind. The trident controls the mind using the three forks or prongs representing the three means: pranayama, pratyahara and dharana. This point is made in Goswami's book, *Laya Yoga* and is replicated in Susan Shumsky's book, *Exploring Chakras*. We can reflect on the impossibility of controlling a restless mind by our own will. Many have tried and have failed to control the turbulent ocean of mind; however, using the power of Rakini which lies within us will bear fruit in the same way that addicts cannot release themselves from their addiction until they fall on their knees and surrender to a higher power.

Lotus: This symbolizes the atman in the heart.

Damaru: This represents the *Shabda Brahman*, which is the sound within the silence of nada, the supreme consciousness otherwise known as *Nada Brahman*.

Chisel: This is used to remove ignorance. Within ourselves is the capacity to remove our ignorance by tuning into our own Rakini aspect. Rakini is within us. What we must do is this: access that part of our inner personality, that Rakini aspect, and find the way to sculpt our personality so that we become perfect human beings. Then we can pass through swadhisthana to the next hurdle, manipura. However, it is not possible for us to see what needs sculpting and what does not. The excesses of ahamkara always appear justified, right and correct to the person identifying with them. Therefore, the sadhaka must stay on the spiritual path while the Higher Consciousness, in the form of the presiding goddess of swadhisthana, Rakini, puts us through the lessons of life and gradually sculpts away at our excesses. It is important to any sculptor that his rock does not move and in the same way, the kundalini sadhaka must be steadfast in the quest to pass through swadhisthana for as long as it is takes.

Different depictions of Rakini

8

Planes of Experience

Kosha

We are not just a physical body. We have five bodies, *koshas*, containers, sheaths or subtle bodies: the *annamaya kosha* relating to the mooladhara chakra and the physical body; the *pranamaya kosha* or pranic body relating to the swadhisthana and manipura chakras; *manomaya kosha* or mental body relating to the anahata chakra; *vijnanamaya kosha* or astral body relating to the vishuddhi chakra, and the *anandamaya kosha* or bliss body relating to the ajna chakra. These are the levels of subtle bodies that we have, that are in existence. Swadhisthana is contained within the pranamaya kosha or pranic body.

Swadhisthana and manipura operate through the consciousness of pranamaya kosha. Pranamaya kosha is the first level of subtle or non-physical bodies, and the pranas flow through it. This explains 'phantom pain' and feelings that seem to be in limbs and body parts that have been removed. This is common in war veteran amputees. Some people who suffer severe phantom pain seek the help of psychologists acquainted with neuroplastic techniques. An example of this is a case where the subject used a mirror image of an arm and hand that had been amputated. By opening and closing the hand, it was as if the missing limb was functioning and the cellular mind in the arm was mobilized, resulting in diminished pain. Simultaneous brain scans demonstrated that energy was being developed in certain centres by simply imagining movement in missing limbs; this energy development was shown to be similar to that generated by the Satyananda Yoga pawanmuktasana series of movements, which remove pain and stiffness in existing limbs.

Desire and koshas

Pranamaya kosha is the source of action. In an earlier section of this book, the futility of identifying with the attainment of desires was extensively discussed. Prana is the means by which we attain desires. First comes the thought, 'I want . . .' and then we mobilize ourselves into the action required to attain the desire. Desire is in the mind, the manomaya kosha, and attainment is in the action, the pranamaya kosha. Desire is a message in the mind and it does not disappear with the action of fulfilment. Imagine a car with a mechanical sensor like our desire-driven mind: all the driver will hear day in and day out is a voice saying, "More petrol! More petrol! More petrol!" Even though the tank is full, the mechanical mind keeps on with its neurotic demands. It is a conflict.

In a similar way, swadhisthana chakra is made up of prana which relates to the unconscious mind. When the unconscious tensions are resolved, the chakra opens up and faces upward because Ma Kundalini has passed swadhisthana chakra; however, until this occurs the conflict remains. The conflict centres around an unconscious mind, with its unrelenting desires and drives at the level of manomaya kosha, demanding pranamaya kosha to fulfil it demands.

Desire cannot ever be satisfied. Swami Satyananda illustrated this point when he wrote in *Kundalini Tantra*, "If the sadhaka understands that desire can never be satisfied in a thousand lifetimes, then kundalini can pass through relatively fast." In essence, there are two separate bodies involved here, manomaya kosha with the desires, and pranamaya kosha trying to satiate the desires of manomaya kosha. It is possible for manomaya kosha to digest a new idea, a new thought, a solution to tension that does not include pursuit of a hope, a wish, an ambition or a purchase! There is a song created and sung by The Rolling Stones that says, 'I can't get no satisfaction, but I try and I try and I try and I try'. The Rolling Stones need a little lesson in pranamaya and manomaya kosha and the role of swadhisthana.

It is very difficult, if not impossible, to eradicate desire. Desires come to the mind like flies to the honey pot. They just come and come. If you have this thing, then you want that thing, and if you have that thing then you want the next thing. You know it! The only way to diminish desires is not to have them. Would you like to have a cold beer on a hot day? If you can't have cold beer on a hot day, then after four or five years you never think about it; it just doesn't come to mind. A man from Australia, a nation of beer drinkers, had just been through the summer in India and he was telling me how much he'd love to go home and have a beer. He was a sannyasa trainee in Munger, India. The diet was simple and controlled. He was ready to leave his divine aspiration to live a life liberated from desires to go back home and enjoy a cold beer on a hot day. I knew of another sannyasin who was ready to jump on a plane and go back to Germany for the taste of delicious apples! Fortunately, they both came to their senses (which is a curious and ironic expression) deciding not to change their life's course for a glass of beer or an apple.

In summary, pranamaya kosha does not have a mind; its directions come from the mind. Manomaya kosha does not have pranic energy so we have to be careful in deciding which desires to pursue otherwise we have to work very hard, maybe for the whole life or infinite lifetimes to try to attain these desires.

Loka

Lokas are defined as 'planes of existence'. In the same way as the koshas define the planes of individual existence or the planes of existence for the different bodies, we have the loka on the macrocosmic or universal level. In other words, kosha and loka are the same. If the individual kosha were to be expanded to represent the level of consciousness for the universe or world, then kosha becomes loka.

The seven lokas that roughly correlate to the koshas are: bhuh loka, bhuvah loka, swah loka, mahah loka, janah loka, tapah loka and satya loka. *Bhuvah loka* is the plane of consciousness related to swadhisthana. Swadhisthana is the second level of consciousness where we choose according to taste. As swadhisthana awakens, our tastes evolve. Tastes are not limited to the tongue. Many people have no ear for music yet have a taste for it and can be moved to rapture by a musical passage. Sensitive artists talk of the taste of certain colours to the point where some colours make their mouths water. The highest taste of all is the taste of divine ecstasy. With higher states of consciousness, the fresh taste of wellbeing accompanies the clarity and cheerfulness of a life in bhuvah loka beyond the close entanglements of the bhuh loka. Then we can declare to nobody in particular, or just to ourselves, "Life tastes good!"

Primordial sound switch

Swami Satyananda mentions in *Kundalini Tantra*, "Awakening swadhisthana acts as a switch for bindu, from where primal sound originates. This is an experience of swadhisthana. Any awakening in swadhisthana is simultaneously carried up to bindu, where it is experienced in the form of a sound body, an important psychic attribute of this chakra." This means that together with the awakening of swadhisthana, at a higher level we experience an awakening in bindu from where primordial sound, the origin of the sound experience, can be heard.

Manifest sound is heard with the ears; it is created by the vibration of air waves. It must have a source. We clearly hear sounds in our mind; every piece of composed music is first heard mentally and then played on an instrument or sung. As with everything in the cosmos, the subtle precedes the gross. Thus the question raised is, "What is the origin of sound?" On an exoteric scale, Indians call the origin of primordial sound Shabda Brahman and on an individual or esoteric level, they call it *bindu*. We can experience primordial sound in bindu, that point on the head under the crown where the curve begins to form, where the twirl of hair is formed and where Hindu brahmins wear a tuft of hair.

Benefits and cautions when awakening swadhisthana

According to tantric texts, there are many other psychic propensities gained through the awakening of swadhisthana chakra. These include, among other things: loss of fear of water, dawning of intuitive knowledge, awareness of astral entities and the ability to taste anything desired for oneself or others. It must be remembered that up to swadhisthana, the consciousness is not yet purified. Due to ignorance and confusion, the psychic powers at this level are often accompanied by maleficent mental attributes. What happens here is that when the aspirant tries to manifest or express through the psychic medium, he can become a vehicle for personal and lower tendencies, rather than for the divine. This is the problem of swadhisthana once we awaken it. With every awakening we attain some kind of psychic capacity or psychic power; however, this power can be harmful and it can also lead to insanity if we can't deal with the negative issues within our unconscious. Ordinary, loving people transform into greedy, malicious despots when given power or position without training or maturity.

Psychological experiments were performed on a group of people playing the board game Monopoly. In the experiment, some players were given the advantage of more income and more moves over the others. Everyone knew it was just a game, and those who had to lose because of inbuilt disadvantages suffered no change in behaviour, yet those who wildly succeeded became quite heartless and greedy in destroying the wealth and status of players not doing well.

Even though we have the power once swadhisthana is awakened, we also have to have the maturity to be able to deal with the thousands of negative issues which we have been storing in the unconscious. In Swami Satyananda's words, "The sum and substance is this – the awakening of kundalini is not a difficult task, but to move beyond swadhisthana is. For that you must improve the general background of your psycho-emotional life. Once you pass swadhisthana, you will not have to face any explosive traumas again; however, there will be other difficulties further on. Kundalini is unlikely to descend again, as it is destined to move up, but the problems you will confront will be concerned with siddhis, and they are more difficult to subdue."

The fact that we are trying to learn about kundalini and swadhisthana indicates that we are more interested in evolution and expansion of consciousness and less interested in pursuing greed and other selfish interests. This aspiration itself is an indication or a sign that we have awakened mooladhara and are struggling with swadhisthana. Having awakened swadhisthana, the full power of selfishness exerts and overwhelms us and once again we become helpless prey to our own base values, therefore we need the guidance of a guru to take us through this very difficult stage in our conscious evolution. To awaken mooladhara we begin with asana, pranayama and meditation. As consciousness develops and we begin to awaken our next level, swadhisthana, our thinking changes and we begin to question our aims, objectives and values in life.

In order to cross swadhisthana we need to have some kind of deep analytical capacity, as well as an understanding of *vairagya*, detachment, so that there will be no attachment to desires. We have to develop an ingrained, deep understanding that desires cannot be eliminated by fulfilling them. Then we can let things go, otherwise, we'll be caught up by ideas, 'I need a few cars, a few houses, a lot of money, beautiful people around me, this thing and that thing and then I will be all right.' Even one chocolate éclair seems to hold the promise of getting a feeling of wellbeing if we just follow the dictates of mental desires. We may think, 'My mind is a bit tired now; if I have one éclair I'll be okay.' So you pop the éclair into your mouth and afterwards, you're exactly the same. Then you pop another éclair into your mouth, or you get another house, another million dollars, and what has changed? Nothing. You simply continue to want and crave more, no matter how much you receive. You must cultivate a deeper understanding to discover the actual, primal reason of your chasing after these things all the time. Ultimately, as Swami Satyananda said just after his panchagni sadhana in 1994, "It is very difficult to get away from desires. One day, however, they just drop away. Can you imagine a mind without desires? Can you imagine this? They drop away."

9

Preparation for Swadhisthana Sadhana

The sadhanas are very easy to teach, and the techniques are easy to describe. There is nothing to stop you from going ahead and practising. However, I would strongly advise that you start with the higher practices of ajna chakra first and concentrate on these. The easiest way to concentrate on any chakra is simply to concentrate on that point. You can feel which chakras have awakened, which chakras are vibrating more strongly, through *Om* chanting in each chakra. You will notice a stronger vibration in some chakras as you are chanting the mantra *Om* in them. You can also ask a friend to lie down on their back and pass your hand over their body. The heat and the energy coming from the chakras can be felt and it will be easy to determine which are a little bit awake and which are dormant.

PRACTICES TO HELP AWAKEN SWADHISTHANA

Locating the chakra

Press the coccyx and then move up about one inch and press again quite firmly into the spinal column with your finger, not too hard, but hard enough so that a residual feeling remains half a minute after your finger is removed. Then go on mentally repeating 'Swadhisthana, swadhisthana, swadhisthana, swadhisthana . . .' while concentrating on the point.

We're locating and bringing about a consciousness of swadhisthana chakra.

Locating the kshetram
Press hard on top of the pubic bone and mentally repeat 'Swadhisthana' again and again with concentration. In this way, we bring about an awareness of swadhisthana kshetram.

SHAKTI BANDHA SERIES

Many people, especially beginners, have stiff muscles and joints. For this reason they have difficulty doing classical asanas. Though the whole *pawanmuktasana* or wind-releasing series is effective in loosening up the body, the following exercises for relieving energy blocks will greatly help the beginner with their asana practice. Even people who regularly do asanas may occasionally feel stiff; these are ideal exercises to remove inflexibility from the body.

What is an energy block? Energy in the form of *prana*, life force, is in present in every part of the body. It should be in a state of flowing freely; however, due to faulty chemical reactions in the body the free flow of this prana is often impeded. This results in stiffness, rheumatism and muscular tension. The *shakti bandha* or energy block-relieving exercises eliminate toxins from the body and ensure that the body's reactions are in balance with each other.

One of the most common malfunctions in the body is the faulty operation of the endocrine system. Scientific experiments carried out in various parts of the world, such as Russia, Poland, France, Germany and India, have conclusively proved that asanas, and especially the energy block postures, are very powerful in harmonizing the endocrine system. Those people who cannot do asanas should do energy block exercises as a minimum to prepare for the practice of asanas and to harmonize the activities of their body.

Nauka Sanchalanasana (rowing the boat)

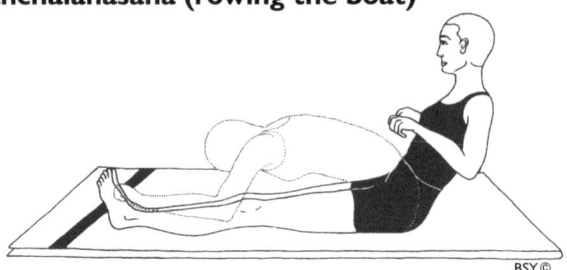

Begin sitting with both legs straight in front of the body.
Imagine the action of rowing a boat.
Clench the hands as though grasping oars, with the palms facing down.
Breathe out and bend forward from the waist as far as is comfortable, straightening the arms.
Breathing in, lean back as far as possible, drawing the hands back towards the shoulders.
This is one round.
The hands should make a complete circular movement in every round, moving up the sides of the legs and trunk.
The legs should be kept straight throughout.
Practise 5 to 10 rounds.
Reverse the direction of the rowing movement as though going in the opposite direction.
Practise 5 to 10 times.

Breathing: Inhale while leaning back.
Exhale while bending forward.

Awareness: Physical – On the movement and sensations in the lower back, hips, pelvic area and the breath.
Spiritual – Swadhisthana chakra.

Benefits: This asana has a positive effect on the pelvis and abdomen and releases energy blockages in these areas; it is particularly beneficial for developing awareness of the muscles and tissues associated with swadhisthana chakra just above the pubic bone. It is especially useful for gynaecological disorders and postnatal recovery. It also removes constipation.

Chakki Chalanasana (churning the mill)

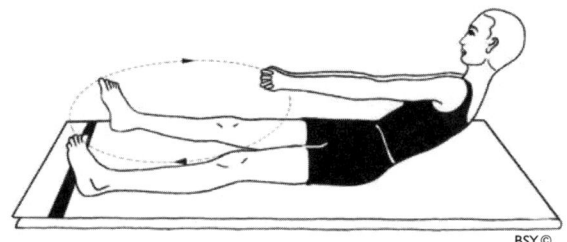

Sit with the legs stretched out in front of the body and with the feet widely separated.
Interlock the fingers of both hands and hold the arms out straight in front of the chest.
Keep the arms straight and horizontal throughout the practice; do not bend the elbows.
Bend forward as far as possible without straining. Imagine the action of churning a mill with an old-fashioned stone grinder.
Swivel to the right so that the hands pass above the right toes and as far to the right as possible without straining.
Lean back as far as possible on the backward swing.
Try to move the body from the waist. On the forward swing, bring the arms and hands to the left side, over the left toes and then back to the centre position.
One rotation is one round.
Practise 5 to 10 rounds clockwise and then the same number of rounds anti-clockwise.

Breathing: Inhale while leaning back.
Exhale while moving forward.

Awareness: Physical – On the movement and sensations in the lower back, hips and pelvic
area and the breath.
Spiritual – Swadhisthana chakra.

Benefits: This asana is excellent for toning the nerves and organs of the pelvis and abdomen. It is very useful for regulating the menstrual cycle and may be performed during the first three months of pregnancy. It is also an excellent exercise for postnatal recovery. This asana massages the uterine and abdominal muscles which are the muscles associated with swadhisthana.

Kashtha Takshanasana (chopping wood)

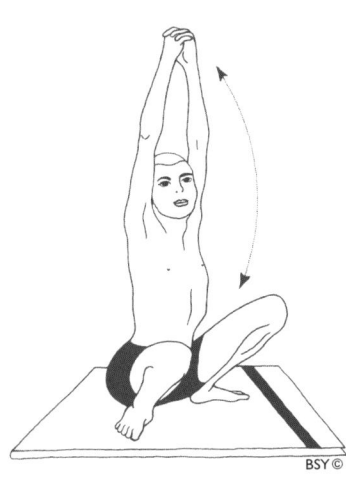

Squat with the feet flat on the floor about 45 cm apart.
The knees should be fully bent and separated.
Clasp the fingers of both hands together and place them just above the floor between the feet. Straighten the arms and keep them straight throughout the practice.
The elbows should be inside the knees.
The eyes should remain open.
Imagine the action of chopping wood. Raise the arms above and behind the head, stretching the spine upward.
Look up towards the hands.
Make a downward stroke with the arms, as if chopping wood. Expel the breath making a 'Ha!' sound. The hands should return near the floor in between the feet. This is one round.
Practise 5 to 10 rounds.

Breathing: Inhale while raising the arms.
Exhale while lowering the arms.
Awareness: Physical – On the movement and stretch of the shoulder and upper back muscles and the breath.
Contra-indications: Not for people with knee problems or sciatica.
Benefits: This asana loosens up the pelvic girdle and tones the pelvic muscles. It also has a special effect on the usually inaccessible muscles of the back between the

shoulder blades, as well as the shoulder joints and upper back muscles. It helps to release frustration and lighten the mood.

Practice note: Those people who find the squatting pose too difficult should practise in the standing position. The benefits, however, will be less.

Namaskarasana (salutation pose)

Squat with the feet flat on the floor about 60 cm apart. The knees should be wide apart and the elbows pressing against the inside of the knees.
Bring the hands together in front of the chest in a gesture of prayer.
This is the starting position.
The eyes may be open or closed.
Inhale and bend the head backwards. Feel the pressure at the back of the neck.
Simultaneously, use the elbows to push the knees as wide apart as comfortable.
Hold this position for 3 seconds while retaining the breath.
Exhale and straighten the arms directly in front of the body.
At the same time, push in with the knees, pressing the upper arms inward.
The head should be bent forward with the chin pressed against the chest.

Hold this position, retaining the breath, for 3 seconds.
Return to the starting position.
This is one round.
Practise 5 to 10 rounds.

Breathing: Inhale while bringing the palms together in front of the chest.
Exhale while extending the arms forward.

Awareness: Physical – On the stretch on the groin and compression at the back of the neck, then changing to relaxation of the upper back and shoulder muscles in the forward position, and the breath.
Spiritual – Develops poise and awareness of swadhisthana chakra.

Contra-indications: Not for people with knee problems or sciatica.

Benefits: This asana has a profound effect on the nerves and muscles of the thighs, knees, shoulders, arms and neck. It increases flexibility in the hips.

Vayu Nishkasana (wind releasing pose)

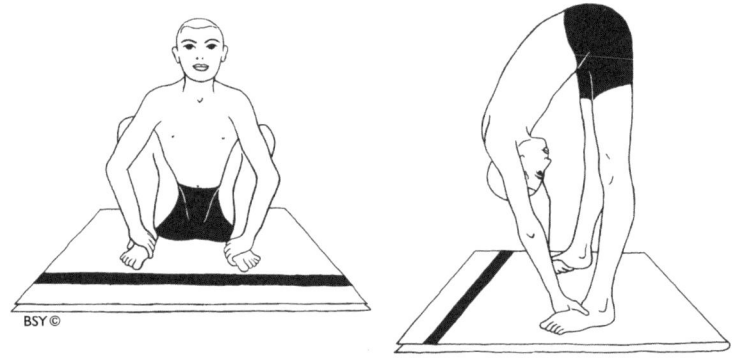

Squat with the feet about 60 cm apart.
Grasp the insteps of the feet, placing the fingers under the soles with the thumbs above.
The upper arms should be pressing against the inside of the knees with the elbows slightly bent.

The eyes should be open throughout the practice.
Inhale while moving the head back. Direct the gaze upward.
This is the starting position.
Hold the breath for 3 seconds, accentuating the backward movement of the head.
While exhaling, straighten the knees, raise the buttocks and bring the head forward towards the knees.
Hold the breath for 3 seconds, accentuating the spinal bend. Do not strain.
Inhaling, return to the starting position.
This is one round.
Practise 5 to 10 rounds.

Breathing: Inhale in the squatting position.
Exhale in the raised position.

Awareness: Physical – On the squatting position, the stretch of the neck in the starting position and flexing of the spine in the standing position, and the breath.
Spiritual – Good for the activation and awareness of swadhisthana chakra.

Contra-indications: Not for people with knee problems or sciatica. People with very high blood pressure or arteriosclerosis should not practise this asana – cautions for inverted postures apply (see *Asana Pranayama Mudra Bandha*, Yoga Publications Trust, Munger, India for details).

Benefits: Like namaskarasana, this pose has a beneficial effect on the nerves and muscles of the thighs, knees, shoulders, arms and neck. The pelvic organs and muscles are massaged.
It gives an equal stretch to the whole spine and both the arm and leg muscles. All the vertebrae and joints are pulled away from each other so that the pressure between them is balanced. Simultaneously, all the spinal nerves are stretched and toned. It is also useful for relieving flatulence.

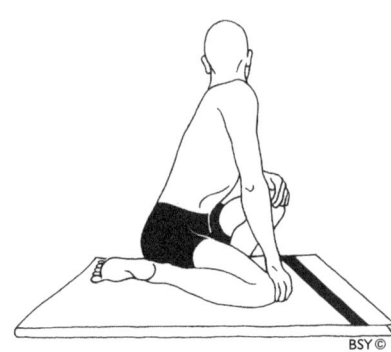

Udarakarshanasana (abdominal stretch pose)

Squat with the feet apart and the hands on the knees.

Inhale deeply.

Exhale, bringing the right knee to the floor near the left foot.

Using the left hand as a lever, push the left knee towards the right, simultaneously twisting to the left.

Keep the inside of the right foot on the floor.

Try to squeeze the lower abdomen with the combined pressure of both thighs.

Look over the left shoulder.

Hold the breath out for 3 to 5 seconds in the final position.

Inhale when returning to the starting position.

Repeat on the other side of the body to complete one round.

Practise 5 to 10 rounds.

Awareness: Physical – On the movement and the alternate stretch and compression of the lower abdomen and on the synchronized breath.

Spiritual – Develops awareness and activates swadhisthana chakra.

Contra-indications: Not for people with knee problems or sciatica.

Benefits: This pose is very useful for abdominal ailments because it alternately compresses and stretches the organs and muscles of this region. It also relieves constipation.

Practice note: Take care not to overstretch the back as the body begins to feel lighter and more flexible.

ASANAS

Shashank Bhujangasana (striking cobra pose)

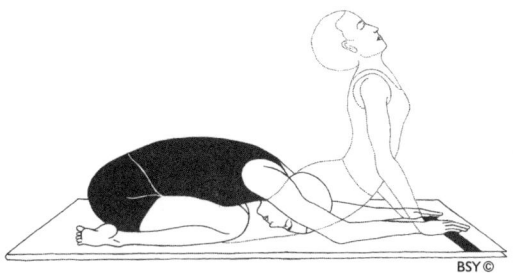

Assume the starting position for marjari asana.
Lower the buttocks onto the heels, moving into shashankasana with the arms outstretched in front of the shoulders.
Then, to come into bhujangasana without moving the position of the hands, slowly move the chest forward, sliding it just above the floor until it is in line with the hands. Move the chest further forward and then upward, as the arms straighten, and lower the pelvis to the floor. Ideally, the nose and chest should just brush the surface of the floor as the body moves forward like the movement of a snake. Do not strain to achieve this.
In the final position, the arms should be straight, the back arched and the head raised as in bhujangasana, even if the navel does not touch the floor.
Hold this position for a few seconds.
Slowly raise the buttocks and move backwards, keeping the arms straight, returning to shashankasana.
This is one round.
Relax the whole body for a short time before starting another round.
Practise 5 to 7 rounds.

Breathing: Inhale on the forward movement. Hold the breath for a few seconds in the final position.
Exhale while returning to shashankasana.

Awareness: Physical – On the flexibility of the spine and the sensation in the arms, shoulders, chest and abdomen; on synchronizing the movement with the breath.
Spiritual – This is an important dynamic asana for awakening swadhisthana.

Sequence: This asana may be practised directly after shashankasana and followed by tadasana.

Contra-indications: Not to be performed by people with very high blood pressure, slipped disc or those who suffer from vertigo. People suffering from peptic ulcer, hernia, intestinal tuberculosis or hyperthyroidism should not practice this asana without the guidance of a competent teacher.

Benefits: Shashank bhujangasana gives similar benefits to bhujangasana and shashankasana. However, the benefits of the latter postures come from maintaining the final position, whereas shashank bhujangasana acts mainly by alternately flexing the spine backward and forward.

This asana gently tones the male and female reproductive organs, alleviates menstrual disorders and is an excellent postnatal asana, strengthening and tightening the abdominal and pelvic region. It tones and improves the functioning of the liver, kidneys and other visceral organs. It also strengthens the back muscles.

Practice note: The hand position should not change throughout the entire practice.

Dhanurasana (bow pose)

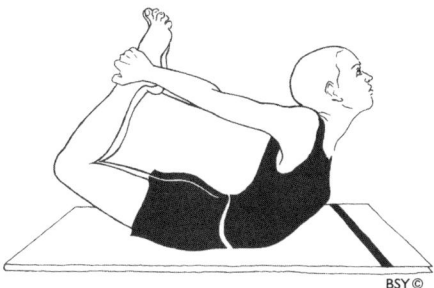

Lie flat on the stomach with the legs and feet together, and the arms and hands beside the body.
Bend the knees and bring the heels close to the buttocks.
Clasp the hands around the ankles.
Place the chin on the floor.
This is the starting position.
Tense the leg muscles and push the feet away from the body. Arch the back, lifting the thighs, chest and head together. Keep the arms straight.
In the final position the head is tilted back and the abdomen supports the entire body on the floor. The only muscular contraction is in the legs; the back and arms remain relaxed.
Hold the final position for as long as is comfortable and then, slowly relaxing the leg muscles, lower the legs, chest and head to the starting position.
Release the pose and relax in the prone position until the respiration returns to normal.
This is one round. Practise 3 or up to 5 rounds.
Breathing: Inhale deeply in the starting position. Retain the breath while raising the body.
Retain the breath inside in the final position or practice slow, deep breathing so that the body rocks gently in unison with the breath.
Exhale while returning to the prone position.

Awareness: Physical – On the abdominal region, the back, or the rhythmic expansion and contraction of the abdomen to the slow, deep breathing.
Spiritual – On manipura, ajna or swadhisthana chakra.

Sequence: Dhanurasana is ideally practised after bhujangasana and shalabhasana and should be followed by a forward bending posture. It should not be practised until at least three or four hours after a meal.

Contra-indications: People who suffer from a weak heart, high blood pressure, hernia, colitis, peptic or duodenal ulcers should not attempt this practice. This asana should not be practised before sleep at night as it stimulates the adrenal glands and the sympathetic nervous system.

Benefits: The entire alimentary canal is reconditioned by this asana. The liver, abdominal organs and muscles are massaged. The pancreas and adrenal glands are toned, balancing their secretions. The kidneys are massaged and excess weight is reduced around the abdominal area. This leads to improved functioning of the digestive, excretory and reproductive organs and helps to remove gastrointestinal disorders, dyspepsia, chronic constipation and sluggishness of the liver.

It is useful for the management of diabetes and menstrual disorders. It improves blood circulation generally. The spinal column is realigned and the ligaments, muscles and nerves are activated, removing stiffness. It helps to correct hunching of the upper back. It strengthens leg muscles, especially the thighs.

Dhanurasana is useful for freeing nervous energy in the cervical and thoracic area, generally improving respiration.

Practice note: This asana must be included in sadhana for raising kundalini shakti into swadhisthana chakra.

Shashankasana (moon or hare pose)

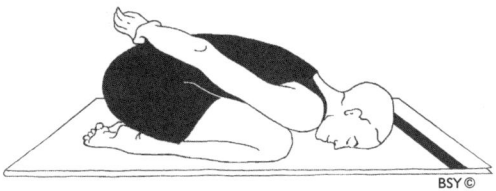

Sit in vajrasana and close the eyes.
Hold the right wrist with the left hand behind the back.
Relax the whole body and close the eyes.
Inhale and then, while exhaling, slowly bend the trunk forward from the hips so that the forehead rests on the floor. Remain in the final position for a comfortable length of time while breathing normally or deeply or in ujjayi.
Return to the starting position while inhaling.

Benefits: This asana tones the pelvic muscles, relaxes the sciatic nerves and regulates the functioning of the adrenal glands, relieving constipation, sciatica and anger. It is beneficial for women who have an underdeveloped pelvis. As swadhisthana awakens, this asana is very effective for removing sexual disorders in general.

Awareness: Physical – In the final position, on the pressure of the abdomen against the thighs; on the alignment of arms, neck and head moving into and out of the asana; on the breath synchronized with the physical movement. Spiritual – On manipura or swadhisthana chakra.

Contra-indications: Not to be performed by people with very high blood pressure, slipped disc or those who suffer from vertigo.

Note: *The Sanskrit word* shashank *means 'moon'. It is derived from two words:* shash *meaning 'hare' and* ank *meaning 'lap'. People in India have seen the dark patches on the full moon as resembling the shape of a hare with the moon in its* *lap. Furthermore, the moon symbolizes peace and calm; it emits soothing and tranquillizing vibrations. Shashankasana has a similar calming and cooling effect. More simply, it is the position frequently adopted by hares and rabbits.*

Paschimottanasana (back stretching pose)

Sit on the floor with the legs outstretched, feet together and hands on the knees.
This is the starting position.
Relax the whole body.
Slowly bend forward from the hips, sliding the hands down the legs. Try to grasp the big toes with the fingers and thumbs. If this is impossible, hold the heels, ankles or any part of the legs that can be reached comfortably. Move slowly without forcing or jerking.
Hold the position for a few seconds. Relax the back and leg muscles, allowing them to gently stretch.
Keeping the legs straight and utilizing the arm muscles, not the back muscles, begin to bend the elbows and gently bring the trunk down towards the legs, maintaining a firm grip on the toes, feet or legs.
Try to touch the knees with the forehead. Do not strain.
This is the final position.
Hold the position for as long as is comfortable and relax.
Slowly return to the starting position.
This is one round.
Breathing: Inhale in the starting position.
Exhale slowly while bending forward.
Inhale in the static position.

Exhale while bringing the trunk further towards the legs with the arms.

Breathe slowly and deeply in the final position or retain the breath out if holding for a short duration.

Inhale while returning to the starting position.

Duration: Beginners should perform up to 5 rounds, staying in the final position for only a short length of time. Adepts may maintain the final position for up to 5 minutes.

Awareness: Physical – On the abdomen, relaxation of the back and leg muscles, or the slow breathing process.
Spiritual – On swadhisthana chakra.

Sequence: This asana should precede or follow backward bending asanas such as setu asana, chakrasana, bhujangasana or matsyasana. (For details, refer to *Asana Pranayama Mudra Bandha*, Yoga Publications Trust, Munger)

Contra-indications: People who suffer from slipped disc, sciatica or hernia should not practise paschimottanasana.

Benefits: This asana stretches the hamstring muscles and increases flexibility in the hip joints.

It tones and massages the entire abdominal and pelvic region, including the liver, pancreas, spleen, urogenital system, kidneys and adrenal glands. It helps to remove excess weight in this area and stimulates circulation to the nerves and muscles of the spine. This is a very powerful asana for spiritual awakening and is highly regarded in ancient yoga texts.

Practice note: Paschimottanasana can also be commenced by inhaling and raising the arms in the starting position, and then exhaling into the forward bend, instead of sliding the hands down the legs.

MUDRAS

Ashwini mudra (horse gesture)
Sit in any comfortable meditation asana.
Close the eyes and relax the whole body.
Become aware of the natural breathing process.
Take the awareness to the anus.
Rapidly contract the anal sphincter muscles for a few seconds without straining, then relax them.
Confine the action to the anal area.
Contraction and relaxation should be performed 10 to 20 times, smoothly and rhythmically.
Gradually make the contractions more rapid.
Awareness: Physical – On anal contraction and relaxation. Spiritual – On mooladhara or swadhisthana chakra.
Contra-indications: People with high blood pressure or heart disease should not practise with *antar kumbhaka*, inner retention of breath.
Benefits: This practice strengthens the anal muscles. It prevents the escape of pranic energy and redirects it upward for spiritual purposes. When contracting the anal sphincter muscle, there is a radiation that goes up inside the spinal column to swadhisthana; this can be felt. When the muscle is released after contraction, the radiation or feeling returns back down again. The contraction is felt up into swadhisthana, with relaxation the feeling returns down.
Note: Ashwini *means 'horse'. The practice resembles the movement a horse makes with its sphincter immediately after evacuation of the bowels.*

Vajroli mudra (thunderbolt attitude) for men
Sahajoli mudra (spontaneous psychic attitude) for women
Sit in siddha/siddha yoni asana, or any comfortable meditation posture with the head and spine straight.
Place the hands on the knees in chin or jnana mudra.
Close the eyes and relax the whole body.

Take the awareness to the urethra.

Inhale, hold the breath inside and draw the urethra upward.

This action is similar to holding back an intense urge to urinate or as if fluid were drawn up a straw. The testes in men and the labia in women should move slightly upward during this contraction.

Confine the contraction to the urethra.

The bottom of the pelvis, just above the pubic bone, is pulled in ever so slightly and this activates swadhisthana kshetram.

Hold the contraction for as long as comfortable, starting with a few seconds, and gradually increasing.

Exhale, releasing the contraction, and relax.

Duration: Begin with 3 contractions, slowly increase to 10.

Awareness: Physical – On isolating the point of contraction, avoiding generalized contraction of the pelvic floor.

Spiritual – On swadhisthana chakra and swadhisthana kshetram.

Contra-indications: Vajroli/sahajoli mudra should not be practised by people suffering from urethritis as the irritation and pain may increase.

Benefits: Vajroli/sahajoli mudra regulates and tones the entire urogenital system. It helps overcome psycho-sexual conflicts and unwanted sexual thoughts. It conserves and redirects energy, enhancing meditative states.

Note: *The word vajroli is derived from the Sanskrit root* vajra, *which means 'thunderbolt', 'lightning' or 'mighty one'. Vajra is also the name of the nadi which conducts sexual energy. Sahajoli is from the root* sahaj, *meaning 'spontaneous'. Vajroli is therefore the force which moves upward with the power of lightning and sahajoli is the psychic attitude of spontaneous arousing.*

CONCENTRATION AND VISUALIZATION PRACTICES

Concentration on the petals

The best way to begin concentration on the petals is to sketch them on paper with coloured pencils. You can start with a bright red or vermilion, six-petalled lotus. Then carefully write the aksharas बंभंमंयंरंलं in white using the Devanagari font. Then become aware of the image through *trataka*, gazing steadily on your piece of artwork. This is the first step and as you continue in this way for some time, a clear image within will ultimately be experienced. This image is to be at the point of swadhisthana chakra, on the spinal column.

The next step is to transform the six aksharas into one mantra, because when you start, you'll start by saying the sounds as individual, separate sounds. With practice, however, they will coalesce into one mantra and not a collection of individual sounds. This is practised with repetition and finally visualize the swadhisthana lotus flower, with the aksharas on the petals, simultaneously performing japa on the visualization, until the whole image becomes steady and stops radiating out.

Visualization of crescent moon

The next practice is to visualize the crescent moon in swadhisthana; continue to meditate on the crescent moon until the crescent moon in swadhisthana comes down to a white point or a white dot, a bright white dot in swadhisthana. Concentration on the moon diminishes down to that.

Concentration on Vam

Concentrate on the bija mantra वं (*Vam*) until Varuna emerges, white in colour, holding a noose of a snake.

Bibliography

Choudhuri, Usha, *Indra and Varuna in Indian Mythology*, Nag Publishers, New Delhi, India, 1981

Dumezil, Georges, *Mitra-Varuna: An Essay of Two Indo-European Representations of Sovereignty*, Zone Books, New York, USA, 1988

Gatwood, Lynn E., *Devi and the Spouse Goddess*, The Riverdale Company Inc., New York, USA, 1995

Goswami, Shyam Sundar, *Laya Yoga*, Motilal Banarasidass, New Delhi, India, 2011

Hackin J. et al., *Asiatic Mythology: A Detailed Description and Explanation of the Mythologies of All the Great Nations of Asia*, Thomas Y. Crowell Company, New York, USA, 1934

Kinsley, David, *Hindu Goddesses*, University of California Press, Berkeley, California, 1986

Nader, Tony, *Human Physiology – Expressions of Veda and the Vedic Literature*, Maharshi Vedic University, Vlodrop, The Netherlands, 1993

Nakamura, Hajime, *A Comparative History of Ideas*, Motilal Banarasidass, New Delhi, India, 1992

Saraswati, Swami Satyananda, *Kundalini Tantra*, Yoga Publications Trust, Munger, Bihar, India, 2002

Saraswati, Swami Satyananda, *Asana Pranayama Mudra Bandha*, Yoga Publications Trust, Munger, Bihar, India, 2008

Shumsky, Susan, *Exploring the Chakras*, Career Press, New York, USA

Weiten, Wayne, *Psychology Themes and Variations*, 7th Ed, Thomson Wadsworth, 2007

Wilkins, W.J., *Hindu Mythology*, Rupa & Co., New Delhi, India, 1982

Woodroffe, Sir John (as Arthur Avalon), *The Serpent Power*, Ganesha and Co., Madras, India, 1997

Notes

Notes